Dawn Breslin's

Power
Book

ALSO BY DAWN BRESLIN:

Zest for Life

Hay House USA: **www.hayhouse.com**
Hay House UK: **www.hayhouse.co.uk**
Hay House Australia: **www.hayhouse.au**
Hay House South Africa: **orders@psdprom.co.za**

Dawn Breslin's
Power
Book

7 Steps to a
Life Makeover

HAY HOUSE, INC
Carlsbad, California
London • Sydney • Johannesburg
Vancouver • Hong Kong

Published and distributed in the United States by: Hay House, Inc., P.O. Box 5100, Carlsbad, CA 92018-5100 • *Phone:* (760) 431-7695 or (800) 654-5126 • *Fax:* (760) 431-6948 or (800) 650-5115 • www.hayhouse.com • *Published and distributed in Australia by:* Hay House Australia Pty. Ltd., 18/36 Ralph St., Alexandria NSW 2015 • *Phone:* 612-9669-4299 • *Fax:* 612-9669-4144 • www.hayhouse.com.au • *Published and distributed in the United Kingdom by:* Hay House UK, Ltd. • Unit 62, Canalot Studios • 222 Kensal Rd., London W10 5BN • *Phone:* 44-20-8962-1230 • *Fax:* 44-20-8962-1239 • www.hayhouse.co.uk • *Published and distributed in the Republic of South Africa by:* Hay House SA (Pty), Ltd., P.O. Box 990, Witkoppen 2068 • *Phone/Fax:* 27-11-706-6612 • orders@psdprom.co.za • *Distributed in Canada by:* Raincoast • 9050 Shaughnessy St., Vancouver, B.C. V6P 6E5 • *Phone:* (604) 323-7100 • *Fax:* (604) 323-2600

Design: Leanne Siu

Library of Congress Control Number: 2004114938

ISBN 13: 978-1-4019-0513-2
ISBN 10: 1-4019-0513-7

08 07 06 05   4 3 2 1
1st printing, August 2005

Printed in the United States of America

This book is dedicated to three uniquely
courageous and inspirational females
in my family:
Mum, Auntie M & Liberty.

Acknowledgements

I would like to thank the following people for their loving support in helping bring this book to life. Michelle, my publisher — I just adore working with you. Reid in the US — it's an honour to have your support and belief in me. Meg & Jo at Hay House UK for your commitment to promoting my message into the media. Florence Hamilton, my gorgeous friend and editor. Jonny Pegg — thank you for your endless support, belief and encouragement. And last but by no means least, Jonny Lawrence — my rock and my earth angel.

Contents

Preface **11**

Introduction **27**
What is this little book all about?

Chapter 1 **41**
Boost self-confidence by 100 percent by taking a big dose of positive self-esteem

Chapter 2 **81**
Quiet your harsh inner critic, STOP being a perfectionist and give yourself the gentle break that you deserve

Chapter 3 **107**
Stuff your emotions down, keep numbing the pain – and miss out on the REAL feelings that you so deserve

Chapter 4   131
*Drop it, let the past go – and grab life
by the tail! You only get one chance*

Chapter 5   153
*Get over your guilt or give up on joy!
You deserve another chance – we all do*

Chapter 6   171
*Bust your fears to embrace your dreams.
Break through this and live your bliss*

Chapter 7   195
*Soul revival! Connect with your sense of
self and dance with life*

Signing off ...   **221**

Further resources   **227**

Dawn Breslin's workshops   **236**

Preface

I believe you deserve to be so happy ...
no matter how you feel right now.
This little book will help.

I BELIEVE that each and every one of us on this planet deserves joy and happiness, yet often we reach points in our lives when we have been knocked back by unhappy and difficult experiences, where we lose sight of this very basic belief. At the same time we also lose sight of how we can ever get back the feeling that we once had. Where did it go? How can we get in touch with it again?

When we are young, our spirits fly high up into the heavens, like a balloon on a gentle windy day. We are carefree, with no responsibilities and no baggage to hold us down. However as we begin to mature and face the trials that every life offers, we can become burdened by what we go through – from marriage breakdown, rape, redundancy, mental and physical abuse to bereavement, illness, disability and all the other physical and emotional upheavals that are inevitable on the path of being human. Usually, as we have never been taught how to handle these situations, we find ourselves just doing the best we can – quietly hoping that we will cope and wishing that one day things will get better.

Our experiences begin to weigh us down, and the balloon that was once flying high can become heavy with baggage, grounding us and making us feel stuck. Often we feel so exhausted that there is no energy to lift us up off the ground again. When we feel this weight, it is often the emotional impact of the experiences that we haven't dealt with, the unresolved emotions that have taken over our free spirit and crushed our joy for life.

Occasionally with a little tipple and in the company of some good friends, our spirits can be rekindled. The next morning, however, we find that the light has gone out again and it's back to the grind of living the routine that has become our lives. In my experience, the only way to ignite our spirits again is to learn how to …

- stop criticizing ourselves and being so harsh to ourselves;
- accept ourselves exactly as we are today, and learn to nurture ourselves;
- realise that we are deserving of love and respect from others;

- let go of past negative experiences that stop us from moving forward;
- address the pains that we have stuffed down and that we haven't faced up to;
- forgive ourselves for our past failings;
- unleash our creative ideas and break through the fears and limiting thoughts that stop us from living our dreams.

If we can begin to work on removing the blocks from our minds, we will access and fully ignite the little spark (our joy for life) that exists in each and every one of us – the spark that never goes out but burns quietly at the core of who we are, patiently anticipating our return. We all deserve to access that potential, and when we learn to take care of ourselves and acknowledge and commit to removing as many of the above blocks as we possibly can, we will then be in a place to nurture our spirits back to life again.

I have worked with hundreds of clients and helped them through this process of releasing and clearing the emotional blockages that are responsible for clogging our spirits and robbing us of the self-esteem and the energy that is essential to nurse our spirits back to life again. In this book I highlight the seven blocks that commonly come up in my sessions.

Try these tests to identify what is weighing your balloon down! Then read the corresponding chapter to gain some insight into the issue. (You might find that you answer yes to questions in more than one chapter – this is natural, as each issue is related to the others.) Make sure that you DO the exercises at the end of each chapter – just reading them won't help.

Nothing will CHANGE unless you DO the work!

Read Chapter 1 –

If you answer yes to any of these questions:

- *Do you feel stuck in a rut?*
- *Do you feel powerless in your life?*
- *Do you feel that you are out of control?*
- *Do you feel confident on the outside but feel your foundations are wobbly?*
- *Do you feel that you do what everyone else wants you to do?*
- *Do you feel worn out and exhausted by your life?*
- *Do you think that expecting real love and respect from others isn't that important?*
- *Is your life a dull routine?*
- *Do you struggle to take time out for yourself?*
- *Do you hold on to the pain of something that you have done in the past?*
- *Do you criticize yourself regularly?*
- *Do you put yourself down in front of others?*
- *Do you allow others to put you down?*

- *Do you feel that you lack courage to make a change?*
- *Do you find it difficult to forgive yourself?*
- *Do you feel like a victim?*
- *Do you look in the mirror and hate who you see?*
- *Do you feel that your life is a life wasted?*

Boost your SELF-CONFIDENCE by 100 PERCENT by taking a big dose of positive self-esteem.

You DESERVE to feel JOY.

Read Chapter 2 –

If you answer yes to any of these questions:

- *Do you feel that your best is never good enough?*
- *Are you frightened of taking risks in case you get it wrong?*
- *Are you confident on the surface but feel weak on the inside?*
- *Do you dislike who you are?*
- *Do you secretly crave deep love?*
- *Do you criticize others?*
- *Do you expect to achieve 110 percent in everything that you do?*
- *Do you criticize yourself harshly if you get something wrong?*
- *Do you continue to push yourself for better results?*
- *Do people always let you down somehow?*
- *Do you avoid creative pursuits because you are not perfect at them?*

- *Would you regard painting as futile because you aren't Picasso?*
- *Do you test people when you meet them?*
- *When you are doing something new, do you have an inner harsh voice that is driving you?*

**QUIET your harsh inner critic.
Stop being a PERFECTIONIST
and give yourself the GENTLE break
that you DESERVE.**

Read Chapter 3 -

If you answer yes to any of these questions:

- *Do you communicate easily about the pain you feel from the past?*
- *Do you feel that you are frightened of dealing with your truth?*
- *Is there secretly something you would like to change in your life, but you are too frightened?*
- *Is there a problem in your life right now?*
- *Is your past haunting you?*
- *Do you need to forgive yourself or someone else?*
- *Do you regularly feel guilty about something?*
- *Is your life out of balance?*
- *Do you shop to feel better?*
- *Do you drink to forget?*
- *Do you drink to relax?*
- *Do you take antidepressants to cope?*
- *Do you take tablets to sleep?*

- *Do you rely on drugs to offer you your 'high' in life?*

Stuff your EMOTION down, keep numbing your pain – and MISS OUT on the REAL feelings of HAPPINESS that you so deserve.

Read Chapter 4 –

If you answer yes to any of these questions:

- *Are you very angry with someone?*
- *Are you angry with yourself?*
- *Do you feel bitter about something from your past?*
- *Do you feel resentful about something from your past?*
- *Do you hate someone?*
- *Do you want to kill someone for what they have done to you?*
- *Do you wish that you could let something go?*
- *Do you feel like you would be weak if you were to forgive someone?*
- *Do you feel that the events of your past are robbing you of your future?*
- *Do you wish that you could change your past?*

Drop it, let the PAST go.
Grab LIFE by the tail ...
you only get one CHANCE!

Read Chapter 5 -

If you answer yes to any of these questions:

- *Do you wish that you could change the past?*
- *Do you wish that you could have said sorry for what you have done?*
- *Do you wish that you hadn't done what you have done?*
- *Do you have huge regrets?*
- *Is the pain of your past creating a void in your future?*
- *Can you forgive yourself for what you have done?*
- *Do you hate yourself?*
- *Do you feel that you deserve to be punished?*

Get over your GUILT or give up your HAPPINESS.

You DESERVE another chance — we all do!

Read Chapter 6 –

If you answer yes to any of these questions:

- *Do you feel like a victim?*
- *Do you feel powerless?*
- *Do you avoid new challenges?*
- *Do you dread change?*
- *Do you secretly admire people who take risks?*
- *Do you fear failure?*
- *Do you fear losing everything that you have worked for?*
- *Do you question how good you are?*
- *Do you worry all the time?*
- *Do you always imagine the worst-case scenarios?*
- *Do you fear change?*
- *Do you avoid change?*

Bust your fears to EMBRACE your DREAMS.

Break through and feel the JOY.

Read Chapter 7 -
    If you answer yes to any of these questions:

- *Do you yearn for your spirit to be free?*
- *Do you want to embrace the joy of life?*
- *Do you want to connect with your creativity again?*
- *Are you living on a treadmill?*
- *Do you feel disconnected from your future?*
- *Do you feel disconnected from your self?*
- *Do you feel like you are just existing?*
- *Do you want to feel so alive?*
- *Do you feel stuck?*
- *Do you wish for a connection with others?*
- *Would you like to have a Zest for Life?*

Get a SOUL revival.

Connect with your SENSE of self DANCING with life!

Introduction

What is this little book all about?

I WANTED to write a book for you that would enable you to get in touch with a sense of the spirit of who you really are. I hope this book will show you how to explore your personal creative power to enrich and lift your life to a better level so that you will feel open to the joys of living and be able to express who you really are in whatever way is fulfilling for you.

In this little book you will have an opportunity to question your inner world of thoughts and feelings, and by doing some gentle clearing work you will begin to unclog your soul and spirit of the obstacles that stop you moving forward. By clearing mentally and emotionally, you will be free to work towards the levels of contentment, joy and success that you truly deserve in this world.

For some, this little *Power Book* will offer an opportunity for personal insight into removing pain and suffering in your life. It is my hope that I can offer you some really powerful tools to repair and recover your sense of self. This will allow you to realise the gift of knowing how important and special you are, no matter what has happened to you in your life and regardless of what mistakes you have made.

See this book as a little companion that has been designed to work with you as a personal friend who accepts you exactly as you are TODAY. The past is in the past and this is your opportunity to stop making any more mistakes; bust your limiting, destructive habits; start to take control of your life; lift your head up high and be proud of who you are in an attempt to move you from where you are NOW into a great new future. The *Power Book* can show you how you to take control of your life ... and your destiny. It can truly work as a tool to set you free to play with the adventure ahead that is YOUR life!

WHAT BELIEFS THIS LITTLE BOOK IS BASED ON ...

The *Power Book* is based on my personal belief that almost every emotion and feeling that we experience on a daily basis comes from a thought that arises in our minds, and somehow if we can dig into the depths of our minds and work out what it is that we are thinking, we will then get some insights into why we are feeling the way that we are.

I also believe that our thoughts are instrumental in shaping the lives that we live. If we have a strong, positive, encouraging internal dialogue that reminds us of how good we are, and how we deserve love, happiness and success in our lives, then love, happiness and success is what we shall achieve. Conversely, if we do not like who we are or we feel that we are not deserving of love, happiness and success, then generally we will not experience them in our lives.

I have been learning to re-programme my thinking for the last ten years and I have moved from a negative, over-sensitive, self-critical mindset to a powerful, self-accepting internal dialogue. I have been surprised at the impact that the awareness of my thoughts and, in turn, my actions have had on my life. It has been amazing how I managed to bring myself from a very depressed state ten years ago into the driver's seat of my life where I am today. I turned my whole life around and conquered so many fears by making my personal self-development my passion, and in this book I explain some of the theories, tools and techniques that I have learned on my journey.

I know that if you make a commitment to put in the hard work and effort, you can do this, too. I have worked with so many clients who have expressed what would make them happy in their lives, and each time we explore their belief structures I find that they have a series of thoughts and beliefs that are blocking them from achieving any kind of happiness. In this book, to ensure that you don't remain stuck in your thinking, at the end of each chapter I have written a selection of affirmations (thoughts and beliefs) that are positive and encouraging and when practised regularly will either offer you a release from the pains of the past or offer you a refreshing insight into an opening for the future.

This little book offers you some really practical tips on how to move from a limiting outlook on life into a more positive state of mind. In the section on fearless living, I will give you a real insight into the mechanics of your habitual thinking processes, to allow you to become more aware of the implications of the way you think and the impact that your thoughts may be having on your everyday life.

I have drawn on my own personal experience as I wrote each part of the book. I also share with you the real experiences of people I have worked with in group workshops or in one-to-one coaching sessions, to allow you to see how the theories relate to real-life situations.

There have been times in my life when I just wanted to read a word, paragraph or a chapter that would shine some light onto a personal issue, problem or difficulty that I was going through. In the *Power Book* I have designed the chapters so that each section offers an opportunity to explore some positive possibilities for change.

When we are knocked back by life's experiences or when we reach a crisis, our self-esteem suffers. I strongly recommend that no matter what attracted you to this book, you should first read Chapter 1.

The secret of boosting self-esteem is the foundation to this book, and I have gone into a lot of detail of how self-esteem is essential as a means to feeling a sense of personal power. I suggest that even if you feel that your self-esteem is intact right now, it will be very worthwhile to dip into this chapter and learn some tools that will enable you to have an enhanced understanding of the issues in the rest of the book, and charge up your self-esteem whenever you feel you need an extra boost of energy.

HOW THE BOOK WORKS

I use the following little formula throughout the book in order to present essential information in quick and easy bite-sized chunks. This means you can pick the book up, look up the section you want, and even if you only have time to read a few pages, the *Power Book* will throw some light on your particular issue or problem. Then when you have a little more time, you can easily come back and read another chapter or two.

The personal story
Gives you a real-life example that you can relate to about the problem.

The problem
Summarises an insight into the problem.

The consultation
Offers an insight into why the problem might arise and what might happen if it is not dealt with.

The prescription
Offers some examples of how to understand and deal with the problem.

The check-up
Offers an opportunity to do a whole range of exercises that will question how serious your problem is, and then offer some practical tips and exercises that you can do to begin to deal with the challenge.

Further help

This section at the end of the book offers a number of follow-up resources to help you deal with the issues you have. It includes a few book titles, workshop ideas and some general information on how to go about getting support and advice, finding local groups, and professional guidance if you feel that's what you need to do next.

THREE THINGS YOU NEED TO KNOW WHEN WORKING WITH THE *POWER BOOK*

The Power Book — a doing book!

The *Power Book* will only work if you are willing to make a change, and change takes hard work and effort. So many people read self-help books, they have an insight — and then forget about it. For this book to work really well for you, you have to DO IT! It's amazing how when we write things down, we can begin to track what we are feeling on a deep subconscious level, and by doing this we have the possibilities of making some monumental mind shifts and making some real life changes.

This is a doing book as well as a reading book. Buy a notebook and work through the exercises and really get to know what is going on in your inner world. Sit back and observe how your thoughts and habits are shaping the life that you are living each day.

Allow emotions to settle before beginning

Every emotion has its season, so be patient as you feel the pain of a difficult experience that you are going through. Often when our emotions are raw, we try to force a change so that we don't feel so bad. When we do this and things don't go to plan, we may give up hope. It is my belief that sometimes you need to sit in the pain of your situation for a bit and allow the emotion to subside before the space for healing can be created. As a bit of time passes and you realise that you are still attached to the pain and the impact of the situation, then begin your inner work with the help of the *Power Book*.

Seek further help if this doesn't work

The *Power Book* is a resource. For some it will give enough theory and insight into the problem to help you let go of the emotion and move on to the next phase of your life. However, if you feel that you have worked through the exercises, done the affirmations with accelerators thoroughly and you still feel that you can't move on after a few months, then make a real effort to go the extra mile and find professional help.

I really believe that everyone deserves the opportunity to live without suffering, certainly if there is a solution for relieving the pain. And there is! At one point in my life I had counselling to work on the beliefs that stopped me moving forward. I couldn't have done it on my own as the pain was buried so deeply. I now feel freer and lighter. It's amazing how removing our emotional blocks can make us feel so different. You deserve this chance, too.

Spring-clean your life and your mind

This little book has been written in an order that will allow you to work through it at random, or you can pick it up when you hit an emotional crisis. The other alternative is to work systematically from beginning to end and do some real emotional clearing — a spring-clean for the mind!

Clearing out leaves us space in our lives to move forward. When we have space in our homes and offices and cars, it allows us to move around and find things easily; we may find that the process of life has more fluidity. Equally, when our spirits are clogged by the thoughts, feelings and emotions that have stuck with us from our past, these thoughts and experiences weigh us down like a lead balloon and it can be very difficult for us to move forward with ease.

Often our inner world is reflected by our outer world. What is your home, cupboard, car, attic, or desk like? Do you need to do some clearing out to create space for the new?

You could make this little book a seven-week/month project and clear a space in your life at the same time as working through each of the seven chapters. Chuck out what you don't need and begin to spring-clean your life TODAY.

Chapter 1

*Boost self-confidence by
100 percent by taking a
big dose of positive self-esteem.*

You deserve to feel joy.

WE CAN only connect to our personal power when we learn to love and respect ourselves. This means liking who we are and recognizing the importance of believing that we deserve to be happy in our lives. It means letting ourselves off the hook for the things that we have done in our past that we feel bad about and allowing ourselves to start with a clean slate ... TODAY.

THE PROBLEM

Low self-esteem

Having self-esteem means feeling good about ourselves; it means we feel worthy of happiness, health, love and forgiveness. When we have healthy levels of self-esteem we have a sense of our strong personal power. Then, and only then, can we dance with life!

I truly believe that understanding how to boost your self-esteem is an essential tool for any kind of inner contentment, happiness or success in life. When our self-esteem isn't intact, we feel frightened and vulnerable, and we are open to life's challenges as they breeze in and easily knock us over, stealing from us the precious joy of our existence on this planet.

If we don't like who we are, if we allow others to walk all over us, and if we feel self-critical and put ourselves down regularly, the impact on our lives can result in a lot of pain and mental anguish which will ultimately manifest itself in low self-esteem.

One of the greatest challenges that I face as a self-development teacher is teaching people to like who they are, and especially if they have had a bad experience in life that has impacted on their self-esteem.

To achieve high levels of self-esteem can take a lot of hard work and practice; however, in this chapter I am going to show you how to get a handle on managing your self-esteem levels, to enable you to make some positive changes and feel so much better about yourself.

All you have to do is to be willing and open to the concepts that I am about to work on with you. This process has worked for hundreds of people – just give it a try. It takes hard work and commitment, but it is so worth it in the end!

Before I had postnatal depression, I never really knew what low self-esteem was. I never needed to know, I guess! When you've got bags of confidence you can fly through life – and I did. I learned, however, that when you don't have it, and you are constantly questioning yourself, believing that you are not deserving of your own joy or happiness, that you begin to feel stuck, insecure and in some ways immobilized. The other scenario is that you are unaware of how you are negatively judging yourself and your life and you just feel that the future has nothing to offer you. This can be a pretty frightening experience; however, what I have learned in the work that I have been doing is that this feeling is much more common than most people would ever like to admit.

It's perfectly natural to experience self-doubt from time to time, and most people do doubt themselves in some shape or form at various points in their lives. Life can be really tough, and when it is, in the ensuing days or weeks or months, and unfortunately for some people, years, we can lose our perspective about who we are and what we are doing on this earth. If we don't recover quite quickly from these doubts, negative emotions and feelings, and if they continue over a period of time, the implications for our health and wellbeing can have some lasting effects.

I have found with so many of my clients that no matter how long the negative and immobilizing feelings have been around, by using some powerful confidence-building techniques, it is absolutely possible to begin to build ourselves back up and get back on track.

In the last five years, I have worked with so many people who felt depressed, anxious, lost, apathetic or stuck in their lives. In most cases when we get to the root of their issues, there is often a real lack of love and respect for themselves, a huge dose of self-criticism or a lack of forgiveness embedded into their thinking. These limiting thinking patterns keep them immobilized and stuck. People expect me, as a personal development teacher, to have bags of confidence, and to a certain degree I do. However the truth of the matter is that like most people, I have days when I doubt myself and I feel low. The difference now is that I know how to manage my self-esteem and confidence levels when they begin to wobble – and boy, do mine wobble sometimes! However, over a couple of weeks, with the routine and practice of some very simple but powerful techniques, I get myself back on track. Hang in there, if you have ever felt like this or if you are feeling like this right now, I'm going to take you through these techniques that I use in this chapter.

With each client I meet it is my mission to help them re-evaluate the way that they see themselves, identify whether they have a positive, loving, and supportive belief system for themselves, and if not, my challenge is to somehow encourage and enable them to think in a new refreshing way. So how do I do this?

THE CONSULTATION

To boost our self-esteem and in turn our self-confidence, first of all we need to become aware of the internal dialogue that plays in our minds. It's a bit like a tape recorder that plays over and over, and if what the tape is playing is negative and critical of you and your life, you aren't going to feel good each day. The good news is that the tapes originate in your mind and you have the ability to change them. Basically what they are is an accumulation of your thoughts, and the point that I am going to make over and over in this book is that our thoughts can always be changed. Let's have a look at the three-step outline to understanding how to manage this process and identify where our self-esteem comes from.

The first step: be aware of your thoughts

It's crucial that we become aware of the destructive thoughts that we have about ourselves. These are the thoughts that are running around in our heads every time we go to do something or every time we open our mouths in front of others to say something. This voice is like a little chatterbox that comments on everything that you do.

The way this chatterbox works is that whatever it says to you will dictate your feelings and emotions; therefore, the first thing that we have to do is become aware of the commands that we are actually giving ourselves on a daily basis. We have to become aware of the implications of how these thoughts are affecting what we do and how we act and interact each day. When we begin to understand how this mechanism works we will be well on our way to making some positive changes.

Let me use an example to help explain this. On a computer, when you key in a bad file command, you won't get what you expect or want on the screen, but if you review this command and type in the right one, you will get exactly the right response and in turn you will be happy.

Let's imagine I meet a client who wants to attract a new partner. If this person thinks *I am too fat and too old to attract a new partner* as a result of this thought (command), they will probably walk with their head down. They might dress in a dull way, they won't put themselves up for fun opportunities that arise and as a result they probably will remain single! This is the negative file command to the brain that results in negative habits and negative experiences.

Ultimately, negative feelings of self-doubt arise and they remain single!

Now let's look at the positive file command. This same person wants to turn their life around. What they need to do is focus on their good points. They need to think: *I am a sexy, attractive person, and I am now going to take all the opportunities that arise to have fun and meet people. I am fun and I like me. I have beautiful eyes and a great bum* (for example!). *I am attracting the right people into my life right now.*

As a result of this powerful internal dialogue, this person's actions change. They begin to go out and have fun and with the right attitude, which makes them feel alive and free-spirited; then they begin to get a different response from the opposite sex. Do you see the difference?

Our minds are just like this — when we think lots of negative, destructive, harsh thoughts about ourselves, we feel vulnerable and weak on the inside, and as a result, we can find ourselves in some really negative and difficult situations in our lives.

So often I hear people say: Why does this always

happen to me? When I search through their belief systems I find, every time without fail, that there is a belief stored in the person's mind that is allowing the negative experience to happen ... it happens over and over, time after time until the negative belief that is attracting negative situations is weeded out.

When we feed our minds with positive, gentle, encouraging and supportive dialogue, we then allow ourselves to feel completely different – this can often offer us immediate physical relief in our bodies and mental relief in our minds. We get in control of what we really want to happen in our lives and start to align our thought processes. Externally, our situations then begin to change for the better. Are you with me? Read this again if you are in any way unsure.

The second step: learn to cultivate some new thoughts

I truly believe that every single human being has an inner core of potential and some fantastic qualities (even if you are thinking to yourself that you don't, my experience tells me that you do. You just haven't worked out what it is yet.)

We all have a light that is capable of shining, and I also believe that it's our deepest desire to seek out our own light and make it shine ... then we learn to play with life!

Remember when you were a child you were like a little balloon filled with helium, free-spirited and flying around in the wind, however as you get older and you go through life's experiences, the balloon gets heavier and heavier until one day it's stuck and weighted down on the ground.

Sometimes over the course of a lifetime, people begin to forget who they really are and how much potential they do have. When we get bumped and bruised by the trials of life, all too often we can forget about our magic and the essence of who we are or who we were born to be. Try this exercise: take out a photo, or close your eyes and remember you as a six-year-old child and look into the eyes of little you! When you do this, ask yourself how you would have liked to see this little being's world shape up.

In my book *Zest for Life*, I use the analogy of people

being just like onions. The centre of the onion has a juicy, sweet-tasting, delicious inner core, and as the onion grows it forms layers, closing the centre in and keeping it safe ... and often stuck. Similarly, as human beings, we also have an amazing amount of potential at our inner core.

Some people say to me that they know deep down that they feel that they could do so much more with their lives but 'stuff' holds them back. Like the onion, humans develop layers, and each time we are bumped or bruised by life, we reassess and change the way we think and react to things. If we are cheated on, we may lose faith in people. If we perceive ourselves to have failed at something, we might believe we are a failure and never try again. If we have a big nose we might think we are ugly and never believe that we deserve a relationship.

Equally, each time that someone says something about us, whether it is a partner, teacher, friend, boss, parent, minister or sibling, we may take on board the comments and allow other people's thoughts to immobilize us in our lives. All too often when we hear someone say something over and over to us, especially if it is negative and against our better judgement, we begin to believe what the person is saying; even although deep down in our heart and soul we know that it's not the truth. Each time we judge ourselves by an experience, each time we try and fail, each time we love and lose, every single time we go through a new experience, we build new belief structures, and depending on what your belief structures are – whether strong and positive or weak and negative – they will determine the outcomes in your life.

So to move on in our lives we need to change our limiting, destructive dialogue and form some positive, supportive dialogue. To do this we use a tool called affirmations. Affirmations are basically short, snappy positive statements that you repeat over and over and over to re-programme your mindset and belief structures. They focus on your deep inner truths and beliefs and they also consolidate all of your positive beliefs. I wish it wasn't so easy to remember all of our negatives, however it's the way the brain works.

If you don't like yourself or your life, the chances are that your life will be miserable

Anna was 39, and for the last twenty years she worked part time, as an admin assistant, in a local insurance company. She married her husband Kevin when she was twenty years old, and they had two children who were now in their teens. The family lived in Kent, and to the outside world Anna appeared to have it all.

I met Anna on one of my workshops, one month before her fortieth birthday. In her own words, she said that she was having a mid-life crisis. I can remember her crying and saying that she felt so selfish for complaining that something was wrong.

Her husband loved her ... but she was bored, her job was safe ... but she was climbing the walls. Her kids were about to leave home ... and she was panicking! Deep down, Anna felt that something was missing ... I suspected very quickly that it was her own sense of self that had gone walkabout years ago.

When I began to work with Anna, she admitted to

me that on a deep level she felt really unhappy, and once we began to peel back the layers of how she felt about her life, she said that she had become the children's mother, her husband's wife, her boss's assistant and her mother's daughter. When I asked her how she would like to feel, she said that she would love to feel free and alive again. She wanted to take risks with all sorts of things in her life, but she felt that it was too late and she didn't have the confidence to make the changes.

After seeing me on TV, she immediately booked a workshop that I was holding in London.

Anna's life had become a treadmill of dull routine, and the vibrant girl that she once was had disappeared down the plughole of life! She knew that she would love to do something different with her life, however the prospect of change 'at her age' was daunting and she didn't have a clue where to start.

To get a measure of how low her self-esteem was, I asked her a number of questions about her life and how she felt about herself. Here were some of her daily thoughts.

I hate my job.
I should be happy with my lot.
*I am unhappy in my relationship; I want fun
    in my life.*
I am selfish having these thoughts.
I'm too old to feel sexy.
I would be terrified to try something new.
I am not bright enough to go to college.
I am unattractive and overweight.
*I am everyone's doormat. Nobody thinks of
    my needs.*
I am unintelligent.
I am a useless mother.
I am a frumpy, unsexy wife.
I had my time in my twenties; my fun is over now.
It's too late in my life to make changes.
I hate my clothes and my look; I am frumpy.
*I am past living life to the full; that's for my
    kids now.*
*People would laugh at me if I embarked upon a
    new career.*

I found a woman who was doubting and criticizing every part of her existence. We can see from the thoughts she was having every day that she had closed so many doors to any future possibilities in her life. The negative, critical internal dialogue that she was running around in her head was squashing any spirit or joy that she might feel. Over a number of weeks, we worked out what Anna really wanted from life. When I cracked the pained exterior and when I dug into her dreams and aspirations, she was just like any other human being; she wanted to be creative and play with her aspirations and dreams; she wanted to love fully and to be loved in return. She wanted to look after herself, and she wanted people to respect her limits, she wanted to care for herself both physically and mentally by looking after her diet and body. Over the weeks that followed, we established that she was passionate about jewellery design, so we did some research into costs and procedures for getting her into college. She was amazed at what she found!

From the first workshop session to the last coaching session, it took two months and a lot of hard work for Anna to get her thinking and her habits turned around. I introduced her to the technique of repeating Positive Affirmations (a technique that I will describe in detail, later in this chapter). I managed to get her to change the way she thought about herself and her life. She switched her negative, limiting dialogue for some positive, nurturing and supportive dialogue and when she did this she created some fantastic new energizing thoughts, actions and habits in her life.

Anna began to think in a different way and approach things quite differently from before, and with all her hard work and effort her life turned around. Over the weeks that we worked together, Anna began to observe how the change in her thinking made a complete difference in the way she saw her life, and observed how her emotions could be re-balanced by thinking these thoughts.

I give thanks for my job; it's an ideal opportunity to fund my college course.

I have a fantastic family unit. I love my husband and the girls so much.

We now energize our relationship with creative ideas. Each Friday Kevin and I go somewhere different.

I deserve to love and respect myself and to honour my creative yearnings.

I feel sexy in my new clothes. I now energize my body and soul with healthy food and exciting exercise (salsa and yoga).

I am open to trying new things; this is my precious life and I am going to live it to the full.

I am so creative and I will have so much knowledge and experience for the course at college. I can do this!

I am attractive, and I now honour my femininity by spending time on my hair, make-up and clothes!

I now have boundaries; I make my life a priority, and from today on I deserve this chance.

I am an inspiring mother to the girls; they love the new me!

I am a fantastic wife, and my husband is energized by the new me.

I have reached forty. The door is now open to my fantastic new future. Yipppeeee!

People will admire me for making life changes, I will inspire others to do the same.

So the good news is that even though you may believe that self-confidence and self-esteem are irretrievable commodities that you have lost sight of forever – they are definitely not! Confidence and self-esteem can be achievable outcomes for anyone who is prepared to put in the hard work to find them – even if they are buried at the core of your onion!

I know that this may look really simple and you

might be thinking that changing your thoughts around can't possibly make you feel better. However later in this section I will explain the mechanics of how to turn your thoughts around to re-balance your confidence and self-esteem. Stick with me ... keep reading!

The third step: learn to be gentle with yourself

Begin to gently nurse your energy and spirit back to life with a big dose of TLC. The stress, pressure and pain of being self-critical can often make us feel like a spring that is tight and tense, or we might just feel empty and listless. It's an exhausting and difficult place to be. However, to commit to a programme of recovering your self-esteem and your self-confidence you really do need to begin to take some time out and do a bit of what you love!

I'm feeling frustrated as I write this, as I know how difficult it is to convince women in particular to make time for themselves. Let me explain why it's ESSENTIAL as part of your healing process to do this.

You might feel that you can't make the time for

yourself, as you think that you are not deserving or you are too busy or you might feel that others' needs should come before yours. The danger here is that by thinking this way, you are not allowing yourself the opportunity to do some deep, essential, internal nurturing and healing. If you don't take the time to energize your spirit, you will become like a washed-out rag, with no energy, no creativity and no love for life.

It is an important part of this process of spirit and soul recovery to work on accepting that you deserve happiness, love, time, respect and forgiveness in your life. Once you get into the habit of accepting these points and begin the process, you gradually introduce some little treats of what you love into your life; you start indulging in a little bit of time for yourself; and you can really begin to de-stress, heal and revitalize your tired spirit.

This process will have an impact on everyone around you, as you become lighter, more refreshed and less uptight.

When we begin to de-stress and feed our minds

and bodies with care and tenderness, our creativity and imagination ignite and become active, and we begin to see the possibilities for happiness in our future. It's an amazing process, and it works — however, to begin it often takes a lot of courage, will and determination.

I can remember one client I worked with who blamed her husband for the fact that she was stuck in a rut and she wasn't living her life to the full. The relationship was getting her down and she was on the verge of divorce. I was amazed that after a few weeks of making time for herself, swimming every day, journaling and taking time out with her friends, she told me that her relationship was blossoming.

This is no surprise to me now, as I have watched so many clients gently pamper themselves back to life — on the inside with their positive, encouraging thought processes, and physically by creating 'me time'.

What lights everyone's fire is different. Some people nurture themselves by bubble baths, massages, candles and walks; others choose an afternoon under the hood of a car! Think of what wild and wonder-full or just plain old everyday pleasures you would like to build into your week and your life to gently nurture yourself back to life. If you make a commitment to taking quality time out for yourself to unwind, recharge and energize, it will be so much better for your partner, your family, colleagues and friends. So start to think about what things would energize your soul that you could possibly re-introduce into your life.

THE PRESCRIPTION

Psychologists say that self-confidence is the removal of self-doubt and when we observe people with high self-confidence and self-esteem, we find that they have a strong, positive internal dialogue at work. These people don't allow the inner critical voice to take over their thoughts and emotions. I often meet clients who have been through a life change, whether it be redundancy, marriage, relationship breakdown, rape, mental abuse, a new baby who cries, bereavement, debt, weight gain, illness or injury. They begin to question and doubt themselves, and it's not surprising that if this questioning and doubt continues over a period of time, it can result in stress, anxiety and even depression.

I would say that 90 percent of my clients come along to the *Zest for Life* workshops because they feel that they have lost a sense of focus and control in their lives; they have lost the courage to make the changes that they would like make; they are constantly questioning their self-worth. As a result, they have a loud voice in their head, reminding them of what they aren't good at and how they aren't deserving – instead of a loud voice reminding them of what they are really good at and how they so deserve to do what would make them happy!

My challenge here is to help you change your focus for the better by using the three-step plan above. If you work hard at this and implement the techniques below, you will begin to feel so much better. Research proves that there is an intrinsic link between the mind and the body, and that self- esteem is an essential and extremely powerful medicine that will help re-balance the energy of your mind-body and spirit.

Think for a moment about a time when you have

fallen in love. I find it staggering that when people fall in love, and they feel that someone loves them, cares for them, believes in them, and is attracted to them, they begin to think and feel so differently. When we fall in love, our immune system is boosted and we find that we don't catch colds or viruses so easily. We believe that we can take on any problem, we become more positive and optimistic about life. The energy created from this powerful emotion and strong, positive internal dialogue makes us feel invincible.

When we learn to love ourselves or when we begin to love the things that we do in our life, by making a commitment to loving, respecting and nurturing ourselves, the impact can be just as powerful — mentally, physically and spiritually.

So how do we do this?

Building positive affirmations

By using the technique of building and repeating positive affirmations, you really can begin to feel completely different. These little sentences, when repeated over and over and over, can open the doors to our potentially joyful futures. Think back to a time when you thought, *I am going to get that job; I am going to get that man/woman; I am going to make this happen*. Can you remember a time when you did this? If you did, you were using positive affirmations and when we do this we give off an air of belief and certainty. As a result, people respond to the way we are feeling and we achieve our desired outcome. Subconsciously we have all done it at one time or another.

So this is not a new concept, but instead something that you have probably done before without being conscious of it. Depending on how much you want the change and how hard you are prepared to work at reading your statements over and over, this will determine how quickly you will get your desired outcome.

Below you will find a three-step plan, followed by an explanation of how to use accelerators, to show you how to create some powerful little sentences to re-programme your thinking. I have used affirmations for years now, and whenever I find that I am frightened or having a bit of a wobble, I repeat them over and over to remind myself of all my good, positive points. I do this until the emotion or the fear that I am feeling begins to settle. Don't worry if you feel they're not sinking in at first – the accelerators are what will give them the oomph that you need to believe them. You can work on building your own personal affirmations in the Check-Up section.

This three-step plan is all that you need to compile some powerful, nurturing and positive affirmations that will energize and inspire you, freeing your mind and spirit.

THREE-STEP PLAN FOR BUILDING YOUR AFFIRMATIONS

Step one: how to re-programme your thoughts

- Your new thought has to be in the present tense – Today, Now, Here & Now.
- Your new thought has to be the opposite of your negative thought.
- Your new thought has to offer a sense of excitement and hope for the future.
- Your new thought will inspire you into action.

Negative affirmation:
I hate my life; it's dull and boring; nothing good ever happens to me.

Positive affirmation:
My new life begins today. I have so much to live for. I am open to new opportunities.

Negative affirmation:
I feel out of control; I am scared.

Positive affirmation:
I now take control of my life. This makes me feel so much better. The future is what I make it, and I am open to the possibilities that life offers me.

Step two: how to use accelerators

Accelerators are basically statements or points that support your affirmation and make it more believable. Listed below are some examples of the types of accelerators you might want to use to support your affirmation.

- Compliments that you have received
- The goal that drives you to think your thought
- Reminders from your past when you thought this way
- Common-sense reasons to believe this thought

I would normally write at least four accelerators to support my affirmation, however you may find that the affirmation works on its own or with just one accelerator. Just make sure it's power-full enough to believe.

Here are examples of how they would work with the previous examples.

My new life begins today. I have so much to live for, and I am open to new opportunities.

I remember in 1995 when life was brilliant. I was open to possibilities then.

I want and deserve to be happy again.

I am looking forward to doing my ceramics again.

I know that I have the potential to do well; before this setback I was flying.

It's exciting to think about what might be around the corner.

I now take control of my life; this makes me feel so much better. The future is what I make it, and I am open to the possibilities that life offers me.

I have been here before and turned it around. I know that I can do this!

I am successful, Paul always reminds me of this. I need to explore my creativity again.

I want to live life and enjoy my days; getting in control again helps me do this.

I need to change my attitude TODAY.

I can do this!

Once you compile your personal affirmations, write them down somewhere you can see them every day. You might even want to record them on a tape and play them over and over to yourself. Repeat them over and over until your subconscious mind drinks them up and you begin to feel completely different, or until people begin to notice a change in you! Go to it. You can do this. Create time this week to sit down and build some personal affirmations that will inspire you. The Check-Up section and the ready-made affirmations should offer you a great start.

Step three: check up your self-esteem levels

THE CHECK-UP

MIRROR, MIRROR on the wall.

Look in the mirror for three minutes and list all the feelings that come up as you look.

1. Write down everything that you think and feel, both positive and negative.
2. If you struggle to find positive things to say about yourself, make an effort to list at least one positive quality and write it down (perhaps even if it is something that someone else has said about you).
3. Do this exercise for 21 days at least, listing only the positive things that you see and feel. If you can't do it at the beginning, persevere for 21 days and observe how differently you begin to feel. Really work hard at this one – it can be tough!

I SHOULD enslaves the mind ...
I CHOOSE is liberating.

Make a list of ten things that you feel you should do in your life.

Then circle all the things that are expectations of other people including your partner and your mother (even if they are dead! It's amazing how this one works!).

And also circle the ones that are JUST silly and have no place being on your list. (YOU may be putting unnecessary pressure on yourself here.)

Now make a list of the things that you could choose to do if you really wanted to.

How important is YOUR life?

Make a list of all the things that you do for YOU and only you to make yourself happy on a weekly basis.

- Make a list of all the things that your partner does for himself on a weekly basis.
- Make a list of all the things that your child/children do for themselves or that you organize.

Now list three things that you would love to do on a weekly basis, wild or simple, and consider how you could fit them in to your life. Plan to make at least one happen this week — beware of reminding yourself that you can't because of time. Build this in NOW!

How are your thoughts shaping your life?

Make a list of five thoughts that you have about how you feel about each of the following. Your:

Body
Face
Future prospects
Personality
Love
Relationship(s)
Life
Parenting skills
Health

What do you think your future holds from the things that you have written down? Look objectively and be honest with yourself. How many doors have you closed by thinking these thoughts? What needs to change? Do you need an attitude overhaul?

Remind yourself of how SPECIAL you actually are — it's so easy to forget.

Now dig deep and think back. List the compliments that you have had for each of the following. These can go as far back as twenty years.

Body
Face
Qualities
Skills/talents
Personality
Parenting
Life
Love
Relationship(s)

Now take this list and stick it on your mirror or in your diary and read it each day until you begin to remember the essence of who you are!

A bit of SPARKLE DUST to sprinkle on your life ...

Make a list of five simple things that you would LIKE TO DO for yourself that would make you feel so much better on a weekly basis.

Being GRATEFUL fills us up with warm feelings and refocuses a tired mind.

Make a list of ten reasons why you are grateful to be alive today. Do this exercise for 21 days until you begin to gently and positively reframe your thinking. List the little things to begin with, such as your health, your ability to pay the bills, your flowerpots, your lovely cat, and your children. Try to write a bit of detail in your descriptions to really make them come alive.

Affirmations to boost self-esteem

I clearly express my boundaries.
I respect others.
I deserve to be respected.

I love and accept myself exactly as I am.

Today I do one thing that makes me
really happy. It's okay to feed my
spirit; everyone will feel the benefit.

From today on I let go of the past and decide
not to judge others, and this feels
so much better inside.

From today on I choose to only feed myself
nurturing gentle thoughts; this energizes
my spirit and sets me free again.

I forgive myself for the past.
Today is a new day,
I deserve another chance at happiness.
I would give other people a chance.

Today is the beginning of my new life.
I have the power in this moment to
make positive changes in my life.

I deserve to have deep love in my life.
I freely express who I am.
I am safe and secure in my world.
I really like me!

Chapter 2

Quiet your harsh inner critic,
STOP being a perfectionist
and give yourself the gentle
break that you deserve.

YOU WILL be connected with your personal power on the day that you learn to accept yourself exactly as you are and when you STOP the voice in your head criticizing everything that you do and everyone that is around you.

The perfectionist's story

I remember working with a lady who had had the best public school education; she had a strict father who had outrageous expectations for her both as a child and as an adult. She was in her fifties when I met her and she was earning around £250,000 (U.S. $466,000). She was so successful, so tough, so judgmental, so critical – and so miserable.

THE PROBLEM

Being a perfectionist can come in a whole range of different disguises. Do you set very high standards for yourself? Do you find that things aren't ever quite good enough for you? Perhaps people always let you down by their imperfections? Do you remind yourself that your best certainly isn't good enough?

As a perfectionist you may shackle yourself with the belief that you can only move forward when everything is perfect or the timing is just right. If this is you, then the chances are that you may just be missing out on so much of the fun that life has to offer, and your inner saboteur may be blocking you from experiencing authentic joy.

If you are a perfectionist, your expectations may be unrealistically high. You may think that when you stand up for the first time in public, you should deliver a speech like one of the best speakers in the world. You may have a movie-star impression of the way you want to look and the way you would like to present yourself to the world. You may wish to constantly better yourself and prove that you are the best in your job. And all for what? What is it that you want to get out of it? Acceptance? Do you really believe that you are not good enough? And if so, why – where did this thought come from?

Perfectionists don't allow for learning curves and they don't allow for spontaneity. They are often immobilized as they move in the direction of their dreams, whether it be speaking to a member of the opposite sex in the pursuit of the ideal relationship, speaking in public for the first time or going after their dream job. Perfectionists STOP THEMSELVES before they move forward. They question if they are going to be perfect for the job, or if now is the right time. They want their world to be a place where no mistakes are made and so often this results in lost dreams. What have you missed out on because you felt that you might not be perfect, or others wouldn't be perfect or meet your standards?

When you learn to accept that in every new situation, you can only do your best, and believe that your best is good enough, you will be free to move forward with ease in your life. I can imagine that you may already be thinking that this belief is not what you were taught at school or what you learned as a child; or you may even have a voice screaming in your head that that kind of attitude will get you nowhere in this dog-eat-dog world.

Please be patient and read on! When you accept

yourself exactly as you are this allows your spirit to be free. When you are free, you can embrace your creativity and you will be open to easily take risks, and to enjoy and play with the wonderful opportunities that life is waiting to offer you.

When you decide to stop criticizing yourself and when you give up on absolute perfection, you are open to embark upon new creative projects and experiences, safe in the knowledge that you can deal with whatever comes your way no matter what the outcome may be! I know this may involve a real readjustment in your thinking – but once you really accept the desire to embrace your creative yearnings and experience new adventures in your life, there is always going to be a learning curve to go through.

What that means for all of us is that we will often make mistakes and produce a result that isn't perfect the first time round. Believe me, mistakes are what happen to everyone who embarks on a new life path!

I can imagine the resistance you may be feeling as you read this section – I feel it myself every time I start something new, because I have to go through the learning experience yet again. I know it is a massive shift that I am asking you to consider. But once we learn to adopt this new attitude towards learning and change, we allow ourselves to experience the fullness of our creativity in our lives as we race towards our authentic dreams.

On the other hand, seeking perfection in everything we do and refusing to cut ourselves a bit of slack can be the main reason for blocked aspirations. When our harsh, negative inner critic judges each of our experiences and the people we meet in a rigid PASS OR FAIL way, the impact of this kind of behaviour can be low self-esteem. Do you look calm and confident on the outside and project the picture of perfection to the outside world, yet underneath the surface, your foundations are cracking and wobbling as you scream at yourself to get it right? Be the best, and DARE to make a mistake!

I can remember that when I decided that I wanted to become a self-development teacher, I was so excited about the prospect of helping people turn their lives around, and I knew in my heart that I needed to begin by running workshops and going on TV in order to reach as many people as I possibly could. In my soul I knew that I could do an amazing job – but in my head there was a completely different tape running!

For the first two years I pussy-footed around and blocked out my dreams. I stayed in reliable employment as the fear of breaking out on my own, standing up to speak in public and appearing on TV daunted me. In my mind, I worried as I thought that I would not come over as well as people like Louise L. Hay (one of the top self-development teachers in the world) or Lorraine Kelly (one of the top UK GMTV presenters).

The fear of not being good enough and constantly comparing myself to the people who were at the top of their fields immobilized me until one day I said to myself, 'Enough is enough'. I decided that I must start somewhere, so I gathered a group of friends together and I presented my first workshop. I ran it in my house with a group of three people. I was shaking! I wore a scarf to hide a nervous rash on my neck, and I had a glass of water at my side to stop my mouth drying up!

After five minutes of speaking and experiencing how I was actually overcoming my nervousness, I was off ... people were engaged and my learning curve began! Within five years I was presenting, sometimes to 5,000 people, and my next move this year is to present with Louise L. Hay in the US! It's amazing how the dream would never have become real in my life and how so many people would not have been exposed to my work, if I hadn't gotten over the fear and allowed myself to be imperfect as I learned and grew.

Interestingly, on one of her audio tapes about her first-ever public speaking event, Louise says that she promised herself that no matter what result she achieved, she would be sure that when she was done, she would praise herself for her efforts. She vowed never to criticize herself.

As she presented, she felt that she could have done better, and when she sat down she reminded herself of the things that she would do differently the next time.

I now know from experience that everyone has to start somewhere, and on the whole, people are always nervous when they embark upon something that is new. The myth is that people who are experts don't go through learning curves ... this couldn't be further from the truth!

When we allow ourselves to grow, and we gently nurture ourselves as we would nurture a child, the results can be staggering. Equally, if we criticize and judge ourselves, chances are we might lose sight of our dreams forever.

THE CONSULTATION

The reason you have created your harsh inner critic is to protect yourself from being made a fool of. Part of you doesn't want to receive any criticism and experience rejection: so your inner critic will convince you that something is not worth taking the risk, unless you are 100 percent convinced that it will work out perfectly.

Whatever you are working on, the critic will expect you to be an expert and get it right the first time. Also the chances are that this voice resonates in your mind as you take on projects and constantly question whether you are good enough. The critic is a tough cookie. Can you think of any of the characters in your life who have spoken to you as harshly as your critic?

The next time you find that you're telling yourself something's not worth doing because you can't possibly do it perfectly, listen to the voice of your critic – what is the voice like? Listen to the tone of the voice. Is it scathing, judgmental, angry, or defensive? Begin to familiarize yourself with him/her. Does the voice sound like a parent, teacher, or partner? Listen closely when you hear it about to start up next time.

I have battled for years with the voice of the critic as I remember my father telling me always to do my best, to be brilliant at everything that I did, and reminding me of all the things that I shouldn't do. Although I no longer hear his voice, so many of the messages that I hear were set in stone when I was a child. The irony is that I am now a woman, and my father has been dead for almost 20 years, yet I still live by the old programmed beliefs that I learned 25 years ago! Quite mad, isn't it, but that's what happens to many of us. I am still vulnerable and quite afraid of criticism. However, nowadays I know that even if I am criticized, especially as I play quite a big part in the media, I could handle it, and the hurt emotions would subside shortly after. I know now that if I allowed my negative critical thoughts to perpetuate, I would not be taking the risk of writing this book.

My inner critic has been nurtured over the past ten years and is now like a pussycat. But every so often when a new challenge comes along, the almighty lion begins to roar in my head. The difference now is that I am totally aware of what's happening, and I gently accept and support this powerful being until the voice quiets down. What has your inner critic done to you and what have you missed out on because of it? Who do you think has helped it develop and made it so powerful?

When we are frightened of doing something in case we get it wrong or when we do things and never feel that we are good enough, this can act as a huge block to our creative yearnings. So often the power and strength of the critic stops us from trying something new unless we KNOW that we are going to be brilliant at it the first time.

I often imagine the critic as a perfectionist gremlin, a little armed guard who stands at the door of our life, guarding the door to our future. He's a strong and tenacious character who always likes to win. He will remind you time and time again when you go to embark upon something that you can only do it if you are going to get something 100 percent right the first time. If this is one of your habits, you begin to eliminate so many things from your life that could offer you authentic joy.

So many people that I work with constantly beat themselves up because they feel that they aren't good enough, aren't bright enough, aren't thin enough, aren't the right person or think that now is just not the right time. By being constantly challenged by their inner critic, they put off so many opportunities that lie before them, if only they could get through the door.

I meet people in my work who are washed out and exhausted; they feel their lives are mundane and they feel so worn down by life. Each time when I get to the core of it, I find that they may be aggressively criticizing themselves, and often they are not even aware of the fact that they are doing it. When their doubts started out, they were probably small children.

When the inner critic appears, I imagine it as a tiny little being. As we begin to listen and respond to its criticism, the voice becomes stronger and stronger. As it gets stronger, the voice becomes louder and we begin to beat ourselves up more and more. As this process takes hold, our self-esteem begins to suffer until on the inside our foundations are very shaky and we feel that we have nothing to give the world, or that one day someone will find out the truth about what we are really like. Can you relate to this? When does your process of self-criticism begin?

I firmly believe that to nurture ourselves and bring some colour and joy into our lives, we must unleash our creativity. I feel the simple pleasures in life, if taken lightly, can result in so much joy and happiness – for example painting for pleasure, drawing, singing karaoke, dancing as if you don't care, dating someone completely different from the usual type of person you go for, throwing pots, playing with clay, making things or writing the novel that is tucked away deep inside your soul – anything that you personally find exciting can make a dull, routine life come alive again.

The inner critic has the power to kill our spirits and deaden our joy for life. It is perfectly capable of ensuring that we live safe, boring, creativity-free lives by always making sure that we:

1. Never walk through the door of our dreams unless we know there is no risk of embarrassment or failure involved! How often does that happen? The risk and the striving are what the adventure is all about.

2. Pay the price and know all about it if we do take a risk, as they will criticize and judge us all the way …

3. Push and push and push ourselves to get better results and to perform at our optimum level, always exhausting us and wearing us down.

The critical, perfectionist gremlin pushes us and expects us to be a master in everything we do. It is so unreasonable as it doesn't allow any space and time for growth and the learning stages of childhood or adolescence. How unrealistic is this?

To get back to the story of the lady who was so self-critical – after a few days of working with her she began to soften and we spoke of the impact of judgement and criticism on the spirit, and how it can deaden your energy and your zest for life. She cried. She was so surprised at how, by being criticized by her father all her life, she was now critical of everyone she met. The very character traits that she hated in him, such as judgement, criticism and always pushing her to be better, were now the exact traits that her life was run by.

On the inside she constantly pushed herself and criticized herself. I found out that she didn't think that there was anything beautiful about herself. She had never stopped to think about how she felt as she looked in the mirror. She avoided all emotional aspects of her being as she pushed and marched through her life. Her self-esteem was at an all-time low. Inside she was yearning for love and affection, however all of her behaviours and mechanisms were set up so that most people were put off by her judgmental air.

As we talked over the week, we spoke of opportunities that she missed out on because of the process of elimination that she had developed to assess whether people were good enough or not. She also spoke of the pain that she felt as the loud voice of her inner gremlin boomed in her head. Over the week we began to feed her mind and spirit lots of positive thoughts; we nurtured her with lots of different healing therapies and we gave her genuine compliments to remind her of the qualities that we could see in her. She was touched, and for the first time in years she said that she felt alive again! It was like watching ice melt. She began to look completely different. When she left the programme, she went off with a renewed mindset and now she has a beautiful new man! She says that she is still plagued by her inner gremlin but she says that she tells it to go and find something else to do when he comes around for tea. He is no longer welcome in her life, and as a result, her life works for her now.

It's quite interesting that when we become aware of the voice, we have a choice as to whether to listen to it and give it power over us or we can allow it to be around. By being aware of its intentions we can drop the resistance and anger and just allow it to fade away. It's funny how when we aggressively resist something, it will always come back and haunt us, however if we accept it and maybe give it a different identity, we can begin to release its power.

Each time we judge ourselves, we are doing violence to our selves, until our spirit is worn down, bruised and bleeding or even, at worst, broken. Can you believe that human beings have such a mechanism? So what about you? On a scale of one to ten, how critical are you of yourself? Hopefully, after reading this section, you may now have an idea of how your internal mechanism works, and in the next part of this section I am going to show you how to tame this little monster!

THE PRESCRIPTION

What I have found really interesting in my work is that when people learn to accept themselves exactly as they are and they accept that they can deal with whatever result they produce, their lives begin to change dramatically ... and the only thing that they have really done is that they have made a MENTAL ADJUSTMENT in the way that they think. The day you understand that it is okay for you to make the odd mistake is the day that you will set your spirit free and your creativity will begin to blossom. Do you think that you could do this? If not, why not?

You may not think that it is possible to begin to change the habits that have become embedded into your thinking over all of these years, however like every other thought or belief that you have, this inner critic is something that you have developed as a habit. As I will say over and over again, all habits can be changed by addressing their source ... and the source of your inner critic is your thoughts. Once we find the thoughts and beliefs that aren't supporting you, you can then begin to change your habits and ultimately you can begin to reshape your destiny. Try these three steps to begin to tame your inner critic.

Step one: nurture the critic

To do this we must first of all acknowledge the voice of the critic. Maybe you would like to give it a name or an identity. Did I hear you say your mother-in-law? Surely not! Once you begin to become aware of its presence, remind yourself that it doesn't always tell the truth. Remember that the critic's job is to scare you from making changes and to do this, it will blow up any tiny grain of truth into an unrealistic and outrageous exaggeration. Write down what it is saying to you on a piece of paper and with someone who loves you and supports you, question how realistic what you have written is. Then DUMP the thoughts that don't support you. Make this commitment to yourself, as you deserve LOVE in your life, NOT CRITICISM. The only way to neutralize fear is by sending love, so write a list of positive affirmations that are hugely accepting and read them each day (check out the affirmation section at the end of this chapter).

Step two: quiet the critic

It takes 21 days to make or break a habit. So, for three weeks work hard at turning down the volume of the inner critic. Make a note on your mirror or in your diary to ensure that you don't forget. THIS IS A TOUGH ONE TO BREAK. Develop a mechanism where you only look for the good in others. Then begin to tell people the positive things that you see. Watch people's responses change towards you. As people's responses change, and they begin to treat you in the way that you are treating them, you then have a positive affirmation mechanism beginning to work for you.

Step three: heal the critic

Because your inner critic has been fed so much power, it has become out of control and power crazy. The way to heal and control it again is to nurture your spirit. By indulging in healing therapies, creative pursuits, and gentle pastimes, this part of you will quiet down. Eventually you will begin to feel more peaceful and relaxed, and ultimately there will be space inside you for your spirit to rekindle again.

Choose two things that you could do this week that would begin to nurture your spirit back to life.

THE CHECK-UP

Look at a photo of yourself as a little child (age 6). Look into the eyes of the little you and ask what you need to do to set his/her spirit free again. How does this exercise feel? How does your inner child deserve to be treated? On a scale of one to ten, how harshly do you criticize this little boy/girl? They continue to live inside you. Do you want to crush them or set them free?

Now have the photo blown up and place it by your bedside. Write a little pledge next to it about the commitment that you are going to make protecting him/her.

Judgement is painful, and although we think that it supports us and keeps us in check, it has the potential to crush us and stop us from actually achieving the one thing we desire most. What things would you like to achieve that your inner critic reminds you that you can't do? How unrealistic are the reasons why you don't go for what you really want?

Make a list of all the things that you feel you should do in order to gain acceptance from people around you. Now question these beliefs as if you were supporting someone you love. Who would the person be? Now list all the things that you could do if you choose to.

Whom do you 'secretly' admire? Think of the spontaneous, fun, warm, loving and caring people that you know. They can be people you know, or people from television or people who are dead. Make a list of the qualities you admire. Once you do this, then question each trait one by one to assess what you need to do or change to be more like them. Once you begin to behave like them, you will begin to attract people like this into your life.

Everybody's idea of perfection is different. What is yours? Make a list of the various attributes that make someone perfect – or pretty close! Now assess your answer and question what beliefs you need to change to be a bit more realistic and gentle with yourself ... and others. Now list the benefits of making these changes.

If you had an opportunity to play with a creative pursuit, what would it be? Imagine that you could just try something for a day just for fun. What would you choose? Now question your response if you were to go for it and arrange to do this. What would your inner critic say? Write down your response and work it through either on your own or with someone who supports you. What would be the worst thing that could happen if you were to do something about this today?

Affirmations

Make a list of affirmations and support them with some powerful accelerators, statements or points that support your affirmation and make it more believable. Listed below are some examples of the types of accelerators you might want to use to support your affirmation.

- Compliments that you have received
- The goal that drives you to think your thought

- Reminders from your past when you thought this way
- Common-sense reasons to believe this thought

Make sure that you read them every day until you feel different and people begin to treat you differently.

I am perfect exactly as I am.

I accept myself exactly as I am.

People are doing the best they can with the knowledge and understanding that they have.

Everyone is unique and different and that's okay.

I accept the things about me that cannot be changed; this makes me feel calm.

Today I look in the mirror and I release the need
to judge myself. This sets me free.

Today I live my life to the best of my ability.
I release the need to compare myself
to others.

I love myself and treat myself with
respect. This way my spirit
can be free.

Today I choose not to judge others.
I accept everyone exactly as they are.
They are only doing the best they can
with the knowledge and experience
that they have.

Today, by being gentle on myself
as I face change, I offer myself the
opportunity to blossom
and grow.

I always do the best that I can,
and that is all I can do, and
that's okay!

Today I commit to thinking
loving and nurturing thoughts
about myself and others. This
makes life so rewarding.

Chapter 3

Stuff your emotions down, keep numbing the pain — and miss out on the REAL feelings that you so deserve.

WHEN YOU choose to release your true emotions and feelings about the pain of your past or about what's going on in your life right now, you will connect with your authentic personal power.

THE PROBLEM

As human beings, we have an integral need to feel good. We instinctively choose pleasure over pain,, and this craving in itself is responsible for the downward spiral of the addiction that so many of us experience in our lives. Unhappy feelings often drive us to go out in search of short-term highs or medication to heal our pain. We may spend our hard-earned money on feeding our legal and illegal addictions that give us 'relief' from our gloomy states!

Surely, instead of looking for the temporary hit from an artificial chemical high or the sticking plaster of a drug that changes our chemical state, we need to address the core issues that are making us feel the way that we do. The body and spirit have a natural balance of energy, and suppressing our thoughts and feelings under addictive behaviour and substances can only lead us to knock out our natural balance. We become disconnected from our authentic power, we are often left feeling disconnected from our true selves ... and the people around us!

All too often I hear people say that they have an issue, then they talk incessantly about it one day, and the next day they don't want to go there ... it's the last thing they want to address. In their mind they convince themselves that they have a handle on it. They stop speaking about it and tell themselves that it has gone away forever?!

I have worked with many clients who have tucked away their true feelings. Men generally find it more difficult to express their feelings. So often when I coach men, in the beginning they say they find it difficult to be open with me about what they really feel. All too often men retreat into themselves, feel unable to communicate, and internalize their emotions in the hope that one day the feelings will go away. On one occasion, if the man I was working with hadn't opened up, he might have acted on the suicidal thoughts he was having rather than ask for help.

I have worked with the wives of men who have been made redundant. Usually these men suffer in silence as their self-worth and esteem have taken such a blow. Often they hit the bottle, and their wives either lose their husbands as they knew them before, or they watch powerless to help as they go towards premature ageing and death.

I have worked with people who have been bereaved and are putting a brave face on things; people who have married and regretted it; people who are in marriages that are over and they can't accept the truth ... there are countless examples that I could give you, and all these situations are normal and part of being human.

The challenge is learning how to deal with them as they come along instead of denying what is happening and burying your feelings. One thing is sure — continuous denial will only keep your mind fixated on the problem, and while emotions remain swept under the carpet, there will be no peace of mind or joy in the good things in life.

So to feel whole and content in our lives, we must

seek our own truth, and learn to be honest with ourselves. We need to find the courage to take the necessary action to live authentically, even if this means seeking help to work through emotions, thoughts or feelings that we don't know how to process or handle.

What do you do to 'feel good', make you feel more relaxed or to calm your nerves? Ask yourself the following:

- *Do you drink to relax or forget?*
- *Do the drugs or tablets that you take allow you to escape, give you the 'high' that you need or make you feel better?*
- *Do you take antidepressants to make life bearable?*
- *Do you need tablets to help you sleep?*
- *How many cigarettes do you smoke per day?*
- *Do you have headaches if you don't have your daily intake of coffee or tea?*
- *How do you feel when you see chocolate?*
- *Do you love the buzz of gambling?*

- *Do you make your credit card(s) scream because you cannot resist temptation when you go shopping!*
- *What's your vice, and more to the point, have you ever taken the time to stop and ask ...why?*

If we are lucky, we have strong supportive parents or partners who can help us work through our pain. Alternatively and more usually, one of the only options available to us is a quick doctor's appointment where we may be offered some form of prescribed medicine to numb the pain or to dull the side effects of our daily stresses or our life crisis.

In the UK and US support groups, counselling and therapy are widely available, but usually you have to put some energy and effort into finding what's right for you, but if you're feeling deeply depressed, asking for help can seem too difficult or even pointless. It's usually well worth it, however, as the experience of sharing can be just what you need to begin to see things differently and get you back on track with your life.

One of the hardest things to do is to ask for help, however, and many people feel too embarrassed to admit that something is wrong in their lives. As a result of appearing on morning programmes like *LK Today* on GMTV, I hear from thousands of people who have been holding onto their pain or suffering because they don't want to admit to their feelings, and don't know how to deal with them.

THE CONSULTATION

So how do we cope?

Often the alternative to dealing with our pain and deep-seated truths about how we feel about our lives — whether it's about insecurity, emptiness or unhappiness — is to seek pleasure in some form of distraction, to take away the pain. This is where addiction can slowly but surely become part of our lives and almost take us by surprise when we stop to really think.

Maybe we were hoping for a short-term feel-good remedy for a deep-seated wound, but everyone who has tried this will know that it hardly ever works. While this kind of distraction may feel good at the time, it always has the possibility of turning into an addiction that in turn can harm the body, enslave the mind and suppress our natural spirit from enjoying the experience of our everyday lives. When we become addicted to something, this can take away any sense of power that we may have. It can make us feel insecure, ruin our health, our marriages, and our relationships with others, and we end up being completely disconnected from our true selves.

I am not in the least surprised that we have an ever-growing population of people suffering from some kind of addiction as the pressures of this fast paced society that we live in throws at us so many ways to escape from our pain.

Accessible porn on the Internet, advertisers' constant promotion of sexy alcoholic drinks, a stunning portfolio of ever-enticing chocolate bars and biscuits, cocaine and heroin at ever-accessible prices, and antidepressants being prescribed hastily in the doctor's ever-decreasing time slot! It's no surprise that people opt for the quick fix of a bit of distraction from their everyday lives, however the real worry is when people become so dependent and offer their whole lives to an addiction to totally get away from what they are really feeling.

Once a little dependency grows and takes root, it's often very difficult to stop the impulses of the brain, as it demands more and more distraction to take attention away from the real issues in our lives. The cycle is ferocious until one day the addiction in itself becomes the focus of our attention and we see it as the problem we have to deal with. However, beneath the veil of most addictions there often lies a need to address our emotions and feelings. But so often these emotions and feelings are so deeply buried that we don't know where to start to get back in touch with them.

I find that people on the whole do resist emotions and feelings. We have all developed personal strategies and ways of functioning in life, and while there is nothing wrong with this, these strategies can also turn into defences or barriers.

When our issues are manageable and we know that they can probably be resolved without having to give them too much attention and thought, a little resistance can be understandable and doesn't stop us from dealing with whatever the predicament might be. However, when we continue to stuff down what is troubling our minds and hearts, when we continue to resist our very own truths, long-term issues, deep-seated trauma or pain, over a period of time we may find ourselves feeling constantly depressed, anxious or worried.

Long-term mental health problems are becoming more and more common because we carry on, insisting that we feel fine instead of stopping and recognizing that our lives are fundamentally out of balance; somewhere, something needs some attention. I can't say this too often – it can be very scary to admit that we need help, but it's very often the most important thing we can do for ourselves.

So many of us, especially the men in our society, just block out our feelings, keep them in and don't talk about what we really think or how we really feel ...

expecting our deep-seated emotions, fears and feelings to gradually disappear over a period of time. This won't happen and there can be serious consequences.

It always makes me smile when I hear Dr Bernie Siegel, a cancer surgeon who practices mind–body healing with his cancer patients, joking about the difference in mortality rates between single men versus married men. He says that he is fascinated by how married men live longer than single men. His theory is that love and communication in a marriage are an important ingredient in maintaining good health – share your emotions with someone who cares for you, and live long! Or another way of putting it is if you want to die a slow, lingering death – get married!

So what happens if we don't deal with our emotion? When we keep emotions bottled up and continue to deny our feelings, the energy created from these emotions doesn't actually go away. All we are doing is pushing the thought and the emotion further and further down (suppression) into our subconscious minds, so much so that eventually some people stuff the thoughts or feelings so far inside that they are not even aware of it any more (repression). In this instance it is extremely difficult to address the issue without some sort of professional help or guidance.

When a memory or an experience is resisted within our minds or when we resist or ignore the sign of an emotion or feeling in our bodies, for example, a fast heartbeat, sweaty palms or a pain in your tummy, the energy that the emotion creates is stored up in our physiology (body).

Over a period of time this electromagnetic energy that is being suppressed may settle in the body, resulting in some kind of dis-ease or illness unless it is dealt with.

Think of this ... when we hear that someone who is really close to us is dead and we experience the pain of grief, we may feel empty, worn out like a rag, exhausted and immobilized. Equally, when we experience redundancy, rape, physical or mental violence the emotional torment that each of these experiences can create is like a big wave of emotion, which at some point needs to be released from our bodies.

Most of us need to cry, yell, scream, talk, or do some physical exercise to release the emotional build-up of energy, from going for a brisk long walk in the open air to punching a bag in the gym, kick-boxing, dancing, yoga or tai chi – whatever works for YOU. You can join a support group, speak to a qualified professional or communicate with very close friends or family – although sometimes friends and family have their own emotional problems or agenda, in which case it can be more helpful to confide in someone who is more objective.

In my experience, if the emotion is not released it is very possible that negative and destructive energy that is stored up in the body over a period of time will suck up – almost like a vacuum cleaner – any natural, free-flowing creative energy within you; leaving you feeling empty, immobilized, apathetic or stuck.

Going through these experiences is part of being alive, and we all feel these types of emotion – I know that I certainly do. The whole process starts in our minds, and is distributed through the body. If our emotions are overwhelming or overpowering, this can create huge physical reactions in our bodies. If we don't let the emotion or the feelings out by releasing them, the energy doesn't just go away. Instead it settles over a period of time and is stored within your body.

Releasing our suppressed emotions leaves us as a balanced and clear channel both mentally and physically, allowing our vital energy to flow more freely, so that our spirit can open out and communicate through our whole being.

The following story shows how your potential can open up once you face up to what's really going on 'behind the smile' of pretended happiness and unacknowledged emotions.

If we admit our deep-seated feelings, maybe we will become vulnerable – so maybe it is easier to live a lie?

Diana was a really gentle young Christian client of mine; she had two beautiful children and nervously came along to my workshop because things weren't quite right in her life. She had been on antidepressants for six years and still found herself wanting to cry each day (but couldn't) and she didn't know why.

When we began to look at her life and her lifestyle, I could see that she was married to a very successful husband and they owned a beautiful home in a lovely suburb of London. Like so many people, Diana couldn't work out what was wrong in her life and it had never even occurred to her that there was an issue with her relationship until she started doing the exercises at my *Zest for Life* Workshop.

It was a complete revelation and also quite daunting for Diana when she addressed her real truths.

Diana's husband had always controlled her and put her down. Over a number of years she had pretended to be so happy and wore a mask for the outside world of being the perfect wife. Beneath the surface she had no self-confidence or self-esteem and therefore no spirit or energy to live the life she really wanted to.

Being honest about her true feelings might have meant confronting her husband about his behaviour towards her, and her fear of the ultimate loss of her material security meant that Diana had repressed her emotions since she had been first married. She blamed herself for being miserable. She admitted that she had pushed the issue so far away that she didn't even know it existed.

She said that when she went to church on Sundays, she would pray that her depression problems would be solved but she did not even consider looking into what was really going on in her relationship with her husband. Now that she was able to begin being honest about her emotions, she recognized that there was a problem here that she needed to face up to.

The next stage of Diana's development was going to take a lot of courage, so we worked on her self-esteem issues and gently built up her self-confidence and her spirit to a point that she would be able to deal with her relationship issues. Once she did this, so many pieces of the jigsaw fell into place. Diana's husband didn't divorce her, as she had feared. Instead they went into relationship therapy and over a period of six months things were much better.

THE PRESCRIPTION

To relieve an addiction, first of all we need to understand that within the body we have a natural balance and flow of energy. When we take in addictive substances and begin to behave in an addictive way – for example, compulsive eating, shopping, TV watching – in fact, anything that becomes a habit that we know isn't good for us – into our lives, it immediately alters the flow of pure natural energy.

In the case of alcohol and drugs, these may divert our attention from how we are truly feeling and cause us to cut off from the reality that we don't want to acknowledge. This TEMPORARILY STOPS the noise inside our heads or dulls out any inner criticism, judgement or pain that we feel. In my book *Zest for Life*, I describe how this inner voice or what I call gremlins have the ability to break our confidence and self-esteem.

In most cases the addictive substance or behaviour may TEMPORARILY stimulate positive emotions such as self-expression, emotional communication, sensuous and sexual energy, a sense of power and control – thus creating an illusion of self-control and happiness.

The challenge lies when the substance or the addictive behaviour wears off and we begin to feel even worse than before. When this happens, the inner critic may scream even louder than before as a result of how you were, felt, behaved, when you were on a high ... and the vicious circle continues. The next day to numb the even louder voice we go for more of the same.

The cycle of addiction enhances self-judgement and criticism, therefore to begin to address addiction we need to start with a programme of gentle TLC, non-judgement and self-forgiveness. As impossible as it may seem, to embark on the journey of recovery we must remind ourselves that there are thousands of people who have gone through the addiction treatment process who made huge recoveries. Recovery is often an impossible task on our own, therefore seeking the help of a non-judgemental support group like AA or Al Anon or a therapist with suitable experience is a fantastic first step before it's too late.

THE CHECK-UP

1. List the life experiences that have had the greatest impact in your life, both positive and negative.
2. Have any of these experiences left you with feelings of loneliness, emptiness, unhappiness, sadness, isolation, regret, bitterness or resentment?
3. How often do you experience the following: intense emotions, mood swings, attitude, impulses/desires, addictive compulsions, or body sensations as a response to thoughts?
4. What do you do to forget/block out your emotions?
5. In what way do you blame yourself for these experiences?
6. In an ideal world, how would you love to feel?
7. What stops you from feeling this way?
8. What help could you get to encourage you to address the suppressed emotions that you feel?

9. a) What would stop you from taking this action?

    b) If you were helping a friend in need and this was their problem, what advice would you give them?

10. What would you like to do, and when are you going to do it?

11. Who could you confide in to help you work through this process?

12. Think about your health and wellbeing. If you don't take action, what will your life look like five to ten years from today?

Addiction/suppression affirmations

Make a list of affirmations and support them with some powerful accelerators/statements or points that support your affirmation and make it more believable. Listed below are some examples of the types of accelerators you might want to use to support your affirmation.

- Compliments that you have received
- The goal that drives you to think your thought
- Reminders from your past when you thought this way
- Common-sense reasons to believe this thought

Make sure that you read them every day until you feel different and people begin to treat you differently.

The Serenity Prayer

Lord grant me the serenity to accept
the things I cannot change
The courage to change the things I can
And the wisdom to know the difference

I am now finding the love and support that
I need in my life.
I am in touch with my higher power.

Today I offer myself real love –
no substitutes
Today I am learning new ways to fulfil
my needs in a balanced way.
From today I forgive myself for all that
I have done.

I was always doing the best that I knew
how at the time.

From today I release the need to judge and
criticize myself, thus setting myself free.
I am so grateful for all the wonderful
things in my life; each day I give thanks
and make a list.

I am alive and well; today is the
beginning of my new life. I am free.
Today I take responsibility to
move forward in my life.

I release the pain of the past; today is
a new day. I am free.

I have got so much to live for.
I am in control of my life. I forgive
everyone in my life, including me.
I am free.

Today I am taking time to recognize how
my body reacts to what I feed it.
I look at me as a small child and
commit to love me again.

From today on, I respect myself.

Chapter 4

*Drop it, let the past go —
and grab life by the tail!
You only get one chance.*

IT IS sometimes so tough to let go of the past, however when we learn to do this, we can reconnect to our personal power and move our lives onto a new fantastic level. Forgiveness of ourselves and others opens the doors to so many future opportunities that we truly deserve (I hear you cringe). Learning to forgive ourselves or another human being for something that has hurt or disappointed us in some way in the past has the potential to re-ignite our spirits and allow joy back into our lives again.

Forgiveness and letting go are the greatest acts of self-love, and the only person who stands to gain from letting go of this emotional pain is YOU! Re-read this last sentence over and over until you understand what it means — if you can't understand what I mean by it, the story below might help. I remember hearing this statement for the first time and not being able to get my head around it, however once I managed to understand the theory, I knew exactly what I had to do!

Here is a classic example of how in an instant, someone's life can take a blow and how the pain of holding on to a painful experience has the power to ruin their lives.

Stolen dreams

Shona was moving to Australia to take a fantastic job opportunity. Four weeks before the move, out of the blue, she received a court order to stop her daughters from leaving the country with her.

Her ex-husband had agreed to the move, but at the last minute changed his mind. The case was taken to court and she was not allowed to take her daughters abroad. Her plans were up in the air and she felt a great sense of injustice as her once-in-a-lifetime opportunity was taken away from her.

Shona was so angry that she became washed out and exhausted. She felt like her bubble for life had been burst, and the anger and resentment that she felt towards her ex-husband reached a dangerous level. Her feelings towards him were dominating her thoughts and dictating her emotions, she couldn't get through her day without thinking damaging thoughts, and would swing into deep depressions. She spent her days thinking resentfully of ways in which she could get him back.

What made it worse was that this was so out of character for her; she rarely felt anger and now her life was being dominated by it. Shona felt that she was out of control. People would advise her to let it go – it had happened and she must move on – but she had no idea of how she could do this. She felt like a monster had ambushed her and stolen her joy. Just when she would begin to feel okay, she would have a glass of wine, then the negative thoughts would re-emerge and dominate her conversations with friends and family.

Maybe you think that Shona was right to continue to fight and identify with the anger that she was feeling, however by thinking these angry and aggressive thoughts, Shona thought that maybe somehow she could hurt him. The truth of the matter is that the only person she was hurting was herself and her two little girls, who were witnessing a very unhappy mummy.

THE PROBLEM

It's exhausting being angry, resentful, bitter and ashamed. It takes up so much time and energy and when we really think about it, all it is doing is making our lives miserable. It creates horrible feelings and keeps us stuck in the painful emotions of our past.

When we have been betrayed, hurt or let down by someone, we somehow convince ourselves that by remaining angry, bitter or resentful, we are hurting them by being vengeful. The irony is that the only person you are hurting by holding onto this pain is YOU.

It's all too easy to feel that when people hurt and damage us, they also have control over our minds and lives, but after the event ... the truth of the matter is that they don't. YOU are in control of your life, and in this chapter I will show you that when you learn to forgive, you can strengthen your spirit and allow a space in your heart to welcome happiness and love back in. It IS possible to let go of the ball and chain that enslaves our minds.

THE CONSULTATION

I often think of this negative energy force resulting from anger, bitterness, resentment and shame as being like a great big vacuum cleaner that gets under your skin and begins to suck out any positive thoughts and happiness that you ever felt. Then it begins to suck up all your energy, creativity, and vitality for life until it has totally consumed every part of your joy, and all you are left with is a mind full of negative thoughts and perceptions about life. This is where the problems begin.

When these thoughts take over, they can begin to dominate your life in such a negative way. When they take hold, it's like a big magnet that attracts even more negative situations, pushing us into a relentless negative downward spiral. The only way to stop this process is to first become aware of it and then learn to clear out our negative thoughts and let go of the negative experience from our mind. So how do we do this?

If we don't learn to forgive and let go of the pains that happen to us in our lives and we choose to hold on to the past, it is very possible that the joy that we deserve to experience in our futures will be limited. Somehow we convince ourselves that it's the other person who suffers from our ties with the experience, but believe me – IT'S NOT. IT'S YOU. Once you accept that you are WILLING to forgive, you then need to consider nursing your bruised and tired soul back to life again. This is a call for some SOUL MEDICINE. To do this we need to fill you up with loving thoughts and affirmations, to relax and relieve your mind, and then get you to begin to feed your spirit with some of the things that your heart and soul loves to do – things that you haven't been doing in a while like feeding yourself good nurturing food, lighting candles, taking soothing bubble baths and revitalising long walks, doing creative hobbies, and laughing with friends.

So let's look at how we can begin to make some changes.

THE PRESCRIPTION

'It's not the snake bite that kills us, it's the venom that runs through our veins after the bite that kills us.' Dr. Wayne W. Dyer

It's not the actual event that causes the most pain when someone is betrayed, hurt, abused or let down – it's the endless holding on to the experience in our minds that wears us down, and it's the resulting impact on our thinking and perspective about the future that stops us from moving forward. So how do we let go of our thoughts?

First of all we have to understand that whatever we think about in our minds each day, whether it be positive or negative, it will have an impact on the way we feel. As we cling on to past hurts and pains, we keep the doors to future love and peace firmly closed.

Using the analogy of falling in love, we can see how the reverse of resentment or anger works on our emotions and physiology. When we fall in love, all we can think about is the other person's face, their wants, needs and DESIRES! We are consumed by the emotion, and as a result, people observe how happy we are and they may even comment on how we are glowing! It's almost as if the emotion takes hold like a fire and spreads through our bodies, boosting our immune systems and making us feel on top of the world.

Now let's look at the reverse. When the thought of the person who has crossed you comes into your mind, you may feel anger or bitterness; the thought expands as you run the pictures in your mind of the pains and upset that they have caused you. The images in your mind affect your emotions, and as a result, you begin to feel low, angry or depressed. You push the emotion down further to cope, but the thoughts don't seem to go away. Your body either feels enraged, empty or washed out. In this example, we can see how the emotions that we are feeling are having a negative effect on both our minds and our bodies. Both psychological research and ordinary human experience prove that not being able to forgive weakens the energy of our minds, bodies and spirits.

Here is a plan to help you move towards forgiveness.

Be willing to forgive

Your ego is fighting this battle. It is saying that you should stay offended and hurt and you should continue to fight. However, your willingness to be happy is your key to your future happiness. Therefore, the first step to letting go is to choose to be happy instead of being right, resentful, angry or bitter. By accepting this you open yourself up to healing your spirit and soul.

Drop your sense of perfection

People make mistakes; we are human. I hear about people's guilt every day – the guilt from people who have hurt others and also the pain from those who have been hurt. When you deal with these emotions every day and you realize how inevitable they are in life, day by day you begin to realize that it is all part of life's rich tapestry. We may not intend to hurt someone, as much as we don't think that we will get over the hurt of our past.

The TRICK is to become AWARE of how we can grow from our difficult EXPERIENCES.

Life is ever complicated and often very painful, however if we do not accept that each experience is an opportunity for us to grow, and if we continue to expect perfection in human beings, this will always result in us being let down.

This may be so difficult for you to do, however try to imagine what it must be like being in the shoes of the person who hurt you. Sometimes people's characters are so different from our own and we can't quite understand why they behave the way they do. To try and empathize, think of their upbringing, genetic similarities to their parents, and their life experiences. Try to imagine why they may have done what they did. Sell yourself a compelling defence on their part and then learn to accept it.

By doing this exercise you don't need to compromise your integrity; the exercise is designed to assist you in softening the blow of your pain and it will set you on the journey towards peace of mind.

Change your thoughts today

You can do this by creating some compelling future-based positive thoughts about your life. I have created some powerful affirmations for you at the end of this chapter. With these, you can begin to re-programme your thinking for the better. Remember that what we think about in our minds is what we get more of and what perpetuates and takes over our thinking (remember the vacuum cleaner!)

In your affirmations, make sure to do the following.

1. Use only positive language. Make sure you don't mention names and experiences that you don't want to think about. Let me give you an example here:

From today on, I will not think about Tom cheating on me with Mary for the last five years – I forgive them both.

We may want to use this one, which is much more encouraging!

From today on, I am free from my past hurts. I accept that people are human and we all make mistakes. I now choose to move freely into my future.

2. Use accelerators (compliments, memories, benefits, future goals) to back up your statement and to really reinforce the power of your belief (see Chapter 1).

3. Practise the affirmations every single day (even if you don't believe them at first). Remember that you have been thinking the negative thoughts for weeks, months or even years and

they have taken over your thought processes.
They are dictating all of your behaviours.

Practising affirmations is a bit like going on a diet. You don't lose the weight by stopping eating chocolate overnight. It has taken a long time to get into this bad thinking habit, ao accept that it will take time to get out of it. Don't give up, though. Even if six months down the line a thought or feeling pops up again, just practice the positive thoughts over again. This takes time and effort.

For some people, letting go the past is easier than it is for others, and it may also depend upon what has been done to you. So first give the affirmations a try, and if it doesn't work for you, commit to getting some professional help.

This is your precious life, and you deserve to be free. For your health and wellbeing it is so important that you don't cling on to pain for too long. Research shows that the energy created from anger and resentment creates conditions under which illness thrives – they clog arteries, stiffen joints, tighten muscles, raise the pulse, and also grip the heart and soul. So you have every reason to make sure that you deal with this today.

Please acknowledge that this is your precious life and you deserve to be free of this pain.

Please make the commitment before another five years pass you by so that the opportunities for your happiness that surround you every day are not missed. Re-read this line and consider the opportunities to be really happy that are being blocked out by your emotions.

THE CHECK-UP

Remember how angry Shona felt towards her ex-husband? I worked with her at one of my workshops four months after her court case. She had come along to review her career and was thinking of embarking upon setting up her own business. As we worked through her material, I could still see the anger that she was holding on to from the case. She said that she felt that she had not come to terms with the decision and she still felt a bit sad at the missed opportunity.

We worked on how she could reframe the experience so that she could feel more at ease. After speaking for a while, I could hear her say that on reflection, she realized how much the kids would have missed their dad and how much he would have missed them. We worked on this empathy and helped her to begin to accept the situation, helping to set her free from the horrible thoughts and emotions that she had been experiencing.

There was a bit of a twist to the story, too. Eight weeks after the case she bumped into the most amazing man, whom she was now dating! She now believes that it was fate that she was meant to stay. She was clearly in love. Isn't life odd sometimes!

How would you feel if I said to you let go of your pain and forgive the person who has hurt you right now? Take a breath here if you have to.

As you read this statement, you may immediately feel that by considering forgiving others who have hurt and bruised you that this would be a sign of weakness. Perhaps on some level you may feel that this means that you are the loser in the fight. You may even feel that if you forgive, you will become even more vulnerable, as the strength of the angry emotion that you had been feeling somehow made you feel stronger.

What is your initial reaction when I ask you to consider forgiveness? Do you think: *There is no way that I am going to stop resenting or blaming them after what they have done to me?* Do you feel a resistance in your thinking or a physical reaction in your body when you consider letting go of the resentment or anger that you are feeling? If so, this is perfectly natural. However, I would ask you right now to just observe what level of control this 'thought' or emotion has over you. How painful or uncomfortable is this feeling? On a scale of one to ten, ten being high and one being low, how much would you like to live without this emotion? Imagine if I were to say to you that you could be free of it tomorrow. Would you accept?

Write a list of all the things that you now think as a result of your experience. Then with someone you love or someone who supports you question the statements you have written down that are closing the doors to your future. Now write a whole list of new positive thoughts that will work for you. Stick them on a mirror and remind yourself each day.

Write the defence for the person who has hurt you. Create a compelling case that supports why they might have done what they did. Imagine the voices of the friends and family of this person as they explain why they did the things that they did.

Write a commitment to letting go this feeling and remind yourself of all the benefits if you were to be free of this pain.

Make a list of ten things that make you feel relaxed and happy. Now ... plan them into your diary for the next three months. They will restore your energy, lift your spirits and make you more positive and optimistic. How much do you want to feel better? If your answer is 10 on a scale of 1–10, then commit to taking time out for you TODAY.

Affirmations on letting go

Make a list of affirmations and support them with some powerful accelerators/statements or points that support your affirmation and make it more believable. Listed below are some examples of the types of accelerators you might want to use to support your affirmation.

- Compliments that you have received
- The goal that drives you to think your thought
- Reminders from your past when you thought this way
- Common-sense reasons to believe this thought

Make sure that you read them every day until you feel different and people begin to treat you differently.

I am now moving into my new glorious future.
The future is what I create it to be.
The past is the past and it cannot be changed,
Today I choose to live and take all of
the opportunities that the universe offers me.

My thoughts determine my
emotions; from today on I choose to
think only positive, encouraging thoughts.

I surrender to the JOY of life.

I have so much to live for.

I feel courageous and
optimistic about the future.

I respect myself and commit
to setting myself free again.

I am open to life's possibilities.

I easily let go, and I forgive.

I release the need to hold on to my resentment.

I welcome joy into my heart.

The door to my heart is open.

My future is about to be rewritten.

I am in control of my thoughts
and love it.

I enjoy new ways of thinking.

Chapter 5

Get over your guilt
or give up on joy!
You deserve another chance —
we all do.

WE CONNECT to our power and set our spirits free when we learn to forgive ourselves for what we have done in the past.

Today is the BEGINNING of your new life – if you CHOOSE it to be.

Choosing ten years of personal pain

Here is an example of someone who wasted ten years of her life feeling guilty.

Chloe had been adopted. I met her when she was in her sixties. She was elegant and stunning. In her late teens she had become a fashion model and met her successful, music-business husband who introduced her to life in the fast lane. Chloe's husband believed in her, and he supported her in opening up what became a very successful PR company in London, looking after some rich and very famous clients. Her PR business began to flourish and blossom.

As Chloe's business grew, she became more and more hungry for success, so much so that she began to neglect her husband and family life and after a couple of years he became involved with another woman. As a result, the marriage broke down.

It wasn't until it was too late that Chloe realized what had happened. She had three beautiful children that she loved very much, and she felt a great sense of guilt as she reflected on how her ambition had destroyed both her family and her marriage. Because Chloe had been adopted, the need for a strong, stable and loving family unit was essential to her. After her marriage broke down, the months rolled on, Chloe became depressed and the business began to wind down.

When I met Chloe, she was in an administrative role for a local firm. She had been doing this job for the past eight years. She went to bed at 10pm and was taking antidepressants to relieve her pain for a life lost. She had given up her hope for the future, as the guilt for what she had done in her past consumed her.

THE PROBLEM

Learning to forgive ourselves for something that we have done in the past can be really difficult. Guilt is one of the hardest emotions to release, and it is only when we accept that we are human, and human beings make mistakes, that we can allow ourselves to be free of the heavy chains that trap our spirits when we feel guilty.

Forgiving ourselves and releasing the need to create more pain and suffering for ourselves is an act of self-kindness that has the potential to allow the energy of joy and love into our lives again. We need to treat ourselves as if we were mothering a small child. Somehow we need to understand that we cannot continue to punish ourselves forever for something that happened in the past that cannot be changed.

The past is the past is the past, and the only way to move forward is to let go the pain and release the need to beat yourself up anymore. So many people that I meet find that they are stuck in their lives because of something that they have done in their past, and they REFUSE or don't know how to let it go.

The only way to heal so many of our pains is to begin to truly love and be kind to ourselves, and we do this by sending love to our bruised and battered spirits. GIVE UP criticizing, whipping and judging yourself today. You are allowed to get things wrong as long as you make an effort to learn from your mistakes and make sure that you don't repeat them. You are only human, and keeping yourself in pain is NOT FAIR to you. Make a choice to give it up now; you have created enough pain and suffering for yourself. It's time to breathe life into your world again and set yourself free.

In the sessions that I worked with Chloe, she began to understand why she had been so hungry for stability. I asked her to stand outside her own life and imagine that one of her children had made the same perceived mistakes that she had made in her life. When we did this, she admitted that if her child had made the mistake she would be disappointed at first, but there was no way that she would beat her daughter up for years over it. She would want her daughter to move on.

Standing outside of her situation and imagining how she would support someone in a similar situation gave her the insight that she needed to release the guilt, take some positive steps and move on.

Chloe's life took a brilliant spin for the better, and this year she began modelling for over-50s, joined a comedy-writing club and managed to settle into a new relationship. She also had dinner with her ex and the children — something that she was delighted about! Chloe had to do some tough work to move on, and now she is optimistic and living life to the full again!

Chloe is not alone in making mistakes in her life. I look back at things that I have done in my life and so many of them are things that I cringe about. There is so much that I wish that I hadn't done. I dated people in my past that I shouldn't have. I said things that I shouldn't have. I have treated people with less respect than they deserve because I was a coward. I have punished myself for separating from my ex-husband. I have felt the intense guilt of responsibility for breaking up a family unit. There were times when I was consumed by guilt for what I had done.

My life began to shape up in a way that I didn't want it to ... because that's what happens when you don't deal with your emotions. I found myself closing down to new relationships, I became afraid of commitment, I didn't want to make the same mistakes again – so I shut myself away. I wasn't aware of what I was doing at the time but in the end, seven years later, I realised that I had to change something in my life or I would never move on.

Eventually I saw a counsellor who helped me put my feelings into perspective. She helped me get over the guilt and she enabled me to open up to the possibilities of relationships and commitment again.

I can be objective about these experiences now. I can recognise my failings and weaknesses, learn from them, grow and move on or I can sit down and dwell on the past each day, beating myself up until the day I die. You have the same choices.

THE CONSULTATION

Guilt can be such a debilitating force. It can tie us up in knots on the inside, it can close doors to future happiness, it can crush your zest for life as you continue to punish yourself for the harm that you have done. It's a painful emotion and somehow we convince ourselves that by embracing the pain of guilt we will feel better and more balanced – we feel this is the payback we deserve for the damage that we have done. But where does the payback end? When will you allow yourself to give up the pain?

If you have treated someone badly, if you have betrayed a confidence, if you have cheated on your partner, stolen something from someone, if you have been angry with someone then regretted it, if you have done irreparable harm or you have done something against your better judgement or values, it's often very difficult to stop beating yourself up and get on with your life.

I have worked with people who have decided to give up on life because of the guilt they choose to hold onto. Is this you?

Often people cannot move on after someone has died and they feel they don't deserve to be happy when the other person is no longer there. I have worked with people whose partners have died and they feel guilty as they choose to build a new life. I have worked with mothers whose babies or children have died and somehow they have kept themselves stuck as they felt too guilty to live because the child was dead. In these cases people feel selfish about building a new life. Once again I have had to ask if the issue in question is selfishness or a deadening of the self as they offer themselves NO LOVE?

The truth is that no matter how we define it or analyse its power, guilt is an absolute waste of time and energy. Guilt does no good whatsoever. It can't bring back the dead, it can't change history and what has happened. It can only harm your inner spirit and deaden the flow of energy in your life. It will beat you up and continue to do so until in your mind, you say enough is enough – it's time to stop it. Once you do this it is then time to start being gentle with yourself and LET IT GO. You can do this if you really want to.

You can feel guilty until your death but it cannot change the event that happened, so we are faced with the option of dealing with the situation as best we can, getting on with our lives or standing still forever. The choice is yours and YOU are in control!

Once you make the choice to let go your guilt or shame, you need to begin to nurse and nurture your spirit back to life again. It's almost as if we need to give you some SOUL MEDICINE. To do this we need to fill you up with loving affirmations to relax and relieve your mind and then get you to begin to feed your spirit with some of the things that your heart and soul loves to do – the things that you haven't been doing in a while, like feeding yourself nurturing food, lighting candles, enjoying long walks, creative hobbies, good company or laughter. Make a list of ten little things that you would love to introduce into your life to relax and relieve your spirit. Think of simple pleasures to start with.

THE PRESCRIPTION

Your soul wants you to forgive yourself and let go of the pain that you feel, it wants you to be kind and gentle to yourself. Your soul craves happiness, peace and contentment and when you choose not to forgive yourself it's a hurtful choice instead of a healing one. Be aware that your ego is holding on to the thought that HURTING yourself is the right thing to do – forgiveness means ceasing to actively harm yourself with inner pain; it means letting yourself out of your internal prison and opening you up to peace and calm again.

Four steps to forgiveness

The first step: selfishness vs self-love

So many people believe that they are being selfish by putting their own feelings first. Be aware that to love yourself is the most nourishing thing that you can do for your spirit. It's what allows you to LIVE and EXPERIENCE life instead of existing as a deadened spirit on this planet.

Take out a photo of you as little girl/boy and look into his/her eyes and ask yourself, if you were the parent of this child, would you feel that it was right to trap them in the pain that they are feeling today? What does this child need to grow and move on in their life experience? How could you nurture them back to life and rekindle their spirit?

The second step: do everything that you can to resolve the situation

It is important that we do everything in our power to alleviate as much of the guilt as we possibly can. Sometimes we need to make a phone call to the person that we have wronged, we may need to have a face-to-face conversation, or write a letter to let someone know how sorry we are for what we have done.

It may feel really uncomfortable to do this as you anticipate the reaction of the other person. You may feel that they will reject you. I feel that it is best to swallow your pride, listen to them and take on board whatever they have to say – then you know that you have done as much as you can in the situation.

I often suggest that if the person is dead, we write the letter anyway, allowing ourselves to release the emotion from within and send the message off into the universe. (I often ask people to imagine a guardian angel messenger who is there to speak to you as you write and allow you to hear the response from the person you are contacting.)

The third step: accept it when there is nothing more that you can do

Release the need to judge yourself and have the wisdom to know when there is nothing more that you can do with a situation in your life. At this point, question how much energy you are putting into feeling guilty and ask *why*. If there is nothing more that you can do, maybe now is the time to LET GO.

The fourth step: learn from the experience

There is a great richness that we can take from times that are uncomfortable. Life is our greatest teacher and we grow most when we go through difficult times. I know that my strength of character has been developed by the beating that life has given me. I have had some really difficult and painful times in my life, and it's then that I have grown most. At the time it's uncomfortable, but in retrospect these are my building blocks to the stronger, more accomplished me! I really believe that if we experience something over and over again, life is knocking on our door to teach us something.

THE CHECK-UP

We all have the ability to heal – it's just a matter of questioning whether we are prepared to be as kind to ourselves as to actually allow the healing to happen. Do you think that you could consider letting go of your guilt right now? When I ask this question, how much resistance do you feel (on a scale of one to ten, ten being high resistance, one being low). Take out a photo of yourself as a small child and look into the eyes of your little child as you consider how much longer you are going to stick pins in this little spirit and hurt her for what she has done.

- List five reasons why you feel guilty or ashamed right now.
- List five of the benefits of letting go of the guilt.
- What behaviours do you need to stop to ensure that you don't repeat the patterns again?
- What could you do to relieve the guilt for each of the above situations?
- Write a letter/create a journal of your feelings and begin to write down why you should continue to feel guilty. Imagine that you are writing to a mentor or friend and really go wild and write as much as you can. In a different-coloured pen, record the voice of your friend/mentor and their opinions as you write.

Take out the photo of yourself as a child. Would you really want to close the doors on this child's opportunities to be happy in this life? If your child was in this situation, would you think it was right for him or her to treat themselves the way that you are treating yourself?

Write a strong compelling defence as to why you did what you did. Imagine that you are presenting your case to your guardian angel. What would the angel say to you?

Affirmations to release guilt

Make a list of affirmations and support them with some powerful accelerators/statements or points that support your affirmation and make it more believable. Listed below are some examples of the types of accelerators you might want to use to support your affirmation.

- Compliments that you have received
- The goal that drives you to think your thought
- Reminders from your past when you thought this way

- Common-sense reasons to believe this thought

Make sure that you read them every day until you feel different and people begin to treat you differently.

Lord grant me the serenity to accept
the things that I can't change
The courage to change the things I can
And the wisdom to know the difference.

I love myself.
Today I choose to be kind to me.
I am free.

I accept that I am human, and from today on
I release the need to judge myself.

Today I choose to be kind to me.
I am in the process of nurturing myself
back to life again.
My guardian angel is with me.
Her wings envelop me.

I feel safe.

I feel that it's safe to let go.

*The doors to my future happiness
are now open. I am looking forward
to accepting the joy and abundance that the
universe has to offer me.*

Chapter 6

Bust your fears to embrace your dreams. Break through this and live your bliss.

WE ARE connected to our personal power when we begin to create the life that we truly want to live by releasing our fears and accepting that we can deal with whatever life throws at us.

THE PROBLEM

When we are free from fear, we can truly dance with life! We can make decisions and changes easily; we feel a sense of personal power as we take personal responsibility for everything that is happening in our lives. We feel at ease as we move from one phase of our lives to the next, safe in the knowledge that we will deal with whatever comes up, one way or another! We don't allow other people to block our paths as we follow our hearts' desires on the journey to our wildest dreams.

Living with fear, however, is much more common than living without it. It's perfectly natural for us to feel fear on a regular basis, especially if we are growing and developing and moving forward in our lives – this type of fear is the norm and almost inevitable as we embrace the challenge of something we have never done before – for example, setting up a business or speaking in public.

However if we are not moving anywhere and we feel stuck by the overwhelming power of fear, this is a completely different issue. This is the fear that often arises from low self-esteem, the result of negative harmful thoughts that we are not good enough, not deserving of love, respect or forgiveness. An example of when we might feel frightened is when we are feeling abused, bullied, unloved – when we feel like a victim of life, always reacting to what's happening to us.

This overwhelming fear has the potential to immobilize us, debilitate us and drag us to our knees unless we know how to work through it. It has the ability to keep us stuck, and it can make us feel stressed, anxious and depressed. It robs us of the very energy that we need to be creative and solve our problems. It is terrifying when we feel out of control in our lives, especially when we have no idea of how to get back on track. It can feel like this type of fear arrives out of the blue, through no choice of your own. If this is you – there are lots of solutions on how to work this through, so keep reading!

Fear comes in all sorts of disguises, shapes and sizes. You may experience the fear of speaking to someone, asserting yourself; or you may fear the future, taking a risk in case you fail, succeeding, public speaking, your rising debt, commitment to someone or something, the prospect of being alone, making decisions, ending a relationship, starting a new career, setting up a new business – the list is endless.

As I compiled this list, I questioned how on earth I had managed to face so many of the above fears and changes. My dad died when I was 16, I was the first of my friends to get married at 22, I travelled around the world on my own and was held at gunpoint in Cambodia at 24, I had postnatal depression and felt out of control at 26, I was divorced at 28, I set up my own business at 29, I spoke in public for the first time at 30, I was £20,000 (U.S. $45,000) in debt by the time I was 31, I was appearing on TV for the first time when I was 33, at 34 I was commissioned to write a book when I was told I wouldn't achieve an O-grade English at high school, I am a single mum and have been for eight years, and I moved to live in a new country, away from my family and friends, at 35.

How did I manage to come out the other end alive! The truth is that I have been terrified with fear so many times, and in some ways I guess that feeling the fear is the price that we pay for the joy and the excitement of the journey in achieving our goals. I feel blessed that I now have some powerful tools to cope with the two types of fear that are outlined below.

Low self-esteem

The overpowering fear that attacks you when you lose your sense of self, when you feel that you don't deserve love, prosperity, forgiveness, success, happiness, respect or joy in your life. This is when you feel powerless and out of control, and convince yourself that you cannot cope. Go to Chapter 1 NOW if this is how you feel.

Natural fear of change

My familiar old friend, fear, is a natural reaction to going through any unfamiliar process without a frame of reference in my mind. This is the fear that arises each time you put myself in the position where you take the risk that you may fail — or should I say more accurately, when you produce a result that may be different from the one you expect.

I'm not for a minute suggesting that when you understand fear it doesn't hurt — I still experience these feelings myself! However, once you begin to be aware of how your mind works, when you begin to take risks and move in the direction of your authentic dreams, fear can become familiar, almost a friend that you know will probably pop up on a regular basis.

You can begin to accept it as a natural process that accompanies change and situations that are unfamiliar. When fear becomes something that is familiar to us, and we recognize that we will always be able to deal with the outcome, we can relax a little and allow our creative energy to become unstuck.

If we don't view fear in a positive way, it will always be something that will dis-empower us and have the potential to steal and imprison our dreams and keep us stuck. In this chapter I am going to share with you the tools and techniques that I have used to help conquer fears. These can be applied to conquer any fear, no matter how great or how small.

THE CONSULTATION

It is the thoughts that we think in our minds that create our feelings of fear. I think of them like little streams of consciousness that play in our heads, tapes containing information in words and pictures that might have been made and re-recorded in the same way many times in our lives. More often than not, this is how our fears get reinforced over time. When we feel the embrace of fear, it is a direct reaction to these thought processes. At the same time, the body reacts by producing its physiological responses like a nervous rash, sweaty palms, upset tummy, sick feelings or a dry mouth.

Fears come from our thoughts

Fears arise when we have convinced ourselves that we cannot cope with the outcome of the situation that we are currently facing. So from this we can see that fears are not just bolts of lightning that come out of the blue but in fact they are a reaction to your negative thoughts that are racing around in your head, terrorizing you!

I often describe the fearful thoughts that go on in our heads as being like spiky little gremlins (self-doubts) all dressed up in armour. I imagine them carrying swords, and their sole purpose is to run wild, fight and destroy all of your positive and creative thinking, ensuring that you feel frightened, doubtful and lost.

The danger here is that if the gremlins (self-doubts) take over, then we are left with no positive frame of reference. When we have no strong positive beliefs and no positive thoughts to feed our imagination and creativity, we often find that we cannot find any solutions to our problems. This doesn't mean there aren't any solutions – just that the gremlins are not allowing us access to them at this moment in time.

It's amazing the capacity we have as human beings to deal with what life throws at us. We cope with many things including the deaths of our nearest and dearest and yet sometimes we (our little negative inner voice) convince ourselves that THERE'S NO WAY I CAN DEAL WITH THIS. The power of this thought together with the bodily feeling of fear can be so strong. We are so sure that we can't deal with the outcome of the thing that we are currently frightened of dealing with — especially if it doesn't work out the way we anticipate. Then afterwards, we realize that the worst part of it is the fear itself!

The bottom line is — no matter what the outcome of your situation, you will deal with it! It's amazing how we become resourceful when our backs are up against the wall. Things don't always work out the way we plan, however this is the game of life, and each time we reach a result that is not our anticipated outcome, we learn a new lesson. Those lessons are what build our character, experience and wisdom in life.

The brain wants to stick with what is familiar

Our brains have a real knack of wanting to stay with what is familiar – they don't really like the hard work of change, and when we present them with something completely different from their current range of experience and knowledge ... they almost have a tantrum! The immediate response is to send out the little gremlin soldiers to frighten you, then usually what happens is that all your worst-case scenarios get blown up out of all logical proportion. This happens so that you might consider sticking with what you know and what is familiar.

However, as you know, once you do something once and then you go back to do it again, because there is now a familiar frame of reference, it gets easier and easier and easier until fear begins to take a back seat and eventually gets overtaken by the urge to go forward.

I have met so many people who have thought about following a dream for a single moment and then in that instant, their gremlins have come out and killed off their dream forever. What dreams have your gremlins killed off as you have travelled through life?

Often people share their thoughts with supportive partners, friends or colleagues who help them in battling with their doubts and fears and remind them of all the reasons why they should take the risk towards their dream. Other people share the dream with people around them, only to be reminded by another human gremlin how it could all go wrong! These poor souls have double the fight – so be careful whom you share your ideas for change with. Only share them with people who will fully support you and be positively objective with you.

When clients share their ideals with me about their life, I ask them to list all of their fears. When we actually look at the list and assess the risk, 95 percent of the time the fears were blown way out of proportion. So often fears are nothing more than negative imaginary blocks. So now let's take a look at my story, which will show you that it only takes an instant to CHANGE YOUR MIND.

My business was about to go bust!

A few years ago my business was owed £15,000 (U.S. $25,000) for some training that we had done and the account was six months overdue. One evening my daughter was at her father's, and I was at home alone. I was on my bedroom floor sobbing. Fear had brought me to my knees and I sat in a corner of the room, feeling stunned and not knowing what to do about paying my staff. I had no money left!

In my head I was imagining the horrible scenario of telling the staff that there was no money to pay them. I then imagined them walking out on me and my reputation being in tatters. I thought that once this had all happened I would have no choice but to close my business down. As I played this scenario over and over in my mind, I realized that I was feeling out of control and I became terrified. My purpose, my passion, my reputation – everything that I had ever worked for – all of it was going to be on the line. What on earth was I going to do?

As I sobbed on my bedroom floor, I asked the universe to help me through this difficult time and then, a few minutes later, I had a thought. I remembered that there was a tiny balance on each of my credit cards, and if I were to scrape these balances together, maybe I'd be able to pay the wages. The next day I paid them!

In real terms, when I was thinking logically again, I could have organized an extended overdraft from the bank as they would have accepted my position. My staff were loyal and would have supported me until the whole situation was resolved a few weeks later, as they knew that the payment was imminent.

It's often so difficult when we are in a fearful place to think straight. However, when you are in the position of fear, the gremlins get in, and when they do, they are like a barrier that acts as a block in your mind, so that it often feels like there are no choices left.

THE PRESCRIPTION

In this section I would like to offer a number of ideas that may help you to put fear into some sort of perspective. Consider these.

BELIEVE in yourself

It is so much easier to make a change when our self-esteem is intact. However there are certain situations, such as abusive relationships, that we need to get out of before we will have the space to re-build our self-esteem. When we believe that we are not good enough and that we do not deserve what the future holds, we can become stuck.

In Chapter 1, I work with you to boost your self-esteem and help you to get back into a place of believing in yourself again. When we begin to imagine the possibilities that the future holds, there is a fantastic physiological response that begins to take place. The natural boost that happens when the feel-good endorphins in your brain begin to flow again means that your creativity and vision for life can be re-ignited. When we begin to boost our self-esteem, the wheels are set in motion and begin to change our perception from one of not deserving and negative self-criticism to one of feeling that we really deserve to have love, joy and happiness in our lives.

When we like who we are, when we feel that we deserve to be treated a certain way, then we find it easier to take risks and move on in life. PLEASE go to Chapter 1 now if this applies to you ... and come back here in a few weeks' time.

Attachment/money

I meet so many people who believe that they couldn't live without their partner (even though they are really unhappy), their three-bedroom house, summer holidays, their lovely garden, their flash cars, their monthly salary, their nights out. It is my belief that as long as we stay attached to the material things that we believe make us happy, we will always be fearful about moving forward.

I was born in a little two-bedroom house in a little mining village in Scotland. I spent my childhood walking through the fields and playing in the woods (something I still love to do!). As an adult I go back to the village and I still appreciate the huge value of this little corner of heaven. I now live in England, in a large Edwardian house with beautiful gardens and far too many rooms! However, I know that if my career went pear-shaped tomorrow, I could go back to my mum's house and still be happy. Because of this perspective, I will continue to climb and fly.

Consider this – could your ego handle living in a caravan or going back to the very beginning in your life again? The day you answer YES to this question is the day that you will begin to play with life and do what is right for you. (The chances are that you will not have to do this, but this is the attitude that allows you to move forward and take the opportunities that present themselves in your life.)

To really move forward in life we need to have a light view of attachment. If you awoke tomorrow morning, having lost everything, what would you do to get back into the driver's seat of your life? Would you be capable of starting again? If you have this plan at the back of your mind, when you make changes you will have so much less to lose. Consider what you are attached to.

Listen to your intuition

You have a gut feel about what is the right thing to do in this situation, and the sooner you realise that your instincts are right and you learn to trust your hunches, you can begin to make moves in the right direction. The problem with intuition is that it can be hijacked by the negative gremlins, too, leaving us confused and uncertain.

Take some time to do something that will relax you and that you will enjoy. You may wish to go for a beach walk, take a train journey, spend time in nature, lie in the bath or listen to music. Take some time out, ask the question about what to do and write down your initial response.

Stop blaming everyone else

As long as you blame everyone else for what is not happening in your life, you are not in control. Blaming takes time and effort and it generally goes nowhere. The minute we take control and accept personal responsibility for what is happening in our lives, we bring decisions into our court. This can be a frightening experience, however the consequences of not being in control mean that your life never ever goes the way that you want it to go. Claim your personal power today, STOP expecting everyone else to bring miracles into your life. YOU shape it – because you can.

Master your language

Here are some examples of how the wrong types of thought and language can disconnect you from your power source. If you begin to use this new vocabulary, you will begin to get into control of your life again. So many of the beliefs below are just bad habits that you have fallen into and all of them can be changed as soon as you make the decision to be in control.

I should
I choose to if I want to

It's not my responsibility
I take responsibility for everything in my life

I can't
I will do the best I can

It's a problem
It's an opportunity

Life is a struggle
My life is an adventure

I can't cope
I can cope with this

I hope
I know

I can't
I choose not to

It's not possible
I will give it my best shot

This is a nightmare

I will learn and grow from this experience

Take a look at your language this week. How many of the above statements do you use? Is your language strong and positive or riddled with gremlins that disempower you and make you feel bad?

THE CHECK-UP

Follow through this 10-point plan to assess how great your fears really are.

1. In an ideal world, list things that you would love to change about your life. Beware of the following blocks:

    Time: You can find the time if you plan.

    Money: If you want the change so badly you will need to get creative.

    Low self-esteem: If you learn to like and respect yourself, you will be stronger.

Too old: You are never too old for something your heart desires.

2. List what FEARS stop you moving forward. List as many outcomes as you can possibly imagine that could happen if you were to take this risk.

3. With a close, caring friend, or the voice of your mentor in your mind, circle all the things that:
   - aren't actually true;
   - probably will never happen;
   - are just exaggerations helped along by your gremlins;
   - you have listed that you realistically couldn't cope with – remember that you WILL cope with whatever life throws at you.

4. Write a list of the ten benefits of taking the risk to move forward. Really go into detail here.

5. Write some words to describe how you would feel five years from now if you weren't to take the risk.

6. Make a list of ten things that could go wrong if you were to take the risk and how you

would deal with the situation if things didn't go as planned.

7. Make a note of what your intuition is telling you right now.

8. List 10 action points, stepping stones from where you are right now, to get you to your ideal place. Four of the stepping stones would be after the risk had been taken.

9. Make a list of the people you could tell about the risk. Make sure that they will positively encourage you.

10. Talk through what you have found with a close friend.

Affirmations to bust your fears

Make a list of affirmations and support them with some powerful accelerators/ statements or points that support your affirmation and make it more believable. Listed below are some examples of the types of accelerators you might want to use to support your affirmation.

- Compliments that you have received
- The goal that drives you to think your thought
- Reminders from your past when you thought this way
- Common-sense reasons to believe this thought

Make sure that you read them every day until you feel different and people begin to treat you differently.

I know that I can deal with
whatever comes up in my life.

I am safe; change will make me
grow in character and strength.

I am safe; this is only change.
As one door closes, another door opens.

Fear will always exists until I
create a frame of reference.
Change allows me to grow.

Fear is a natural reaction,
I am in control of my gremlins.

I love and respect myself.
I deserve the best in life.

I am worthy of happiness.

I am in control of my life
and I love it.

From today on I now move into
my fantastic new future.
My new life can be whatever I
choose. I feel optimistic about the
future.

Chapter 7

Soul revival!
Connect with your sense of self
and dance with life.

WE CONNECT to our personal power when we have a sense of purpose in our lives, when we feel a connection with both our sense of self and the greater force that surrounds us. Only then do we feel that our lives are truly worth living.

The therapist who needed soul therapy!

Sometime ago I worked with Karen, who had a demanding job as a drug counsellor. She arrived at my workshop exhausted, worn out and in tatters. She felt that she was deeply depressed and didn't know where to start to get her life back on track.

Each day she would paint on the mask to her family and her clients and project to the world that everything was okay. Each day she would work with her clients, motivating and inspiring them to make changes in their lives. Recently she had begun to feel that the work was no longer rewarding.

As I worked with her, she told me that she suspected that her husband was having an affair and she said that she would have divorced him if it wasn't for her four kids. She felt trapped, unfulfilled, overworked and exhausted. Her life seemed such a mess, and she felt seriously concerned that she was on the verge of a breakdown.

I felt so deeply for her. She was bright and theoretically knew all the answers. I couldn't imagine that I could teach her anything that she didn't already know – her training had been so similar to mine yet she had fallen off the track.

Instead of taxing her already exhausted mind with doing new affirmations and working through her fears, I decided to take a different approach to try to lighten the weight of her world. So we agreed to work on a more intuitive level using soul meditation and intuition techniques.

In our first one-on-one session, I asked her what she specifically wanted to achieve from working with me. She said that she wanted to feel that life was worth living. She really wanted to feel a sense of connection both with her own life and a deeper spiritual connection with her being on this planet. She felt so off track that she had no idea where to begin.

I asked her to begin the process by bringing lots of

different magazines to our next session. I said that they had to be aspirational and had to contain inspirational images and pictures. She brought along a travel brochure, magazines on health, homes and gardens, and a couple of upmarket glossies. It may sound odd, however we had the perfect tools to get started!

When she arrived at my home I gave her the choice of four different types of music and asked her to choose the music that would be most soothing and gentle for her soul at this time. I then offered her four different types of herbal tea — soothing, revitalising, nurturing and energizing.

The two-hour soul revival session began. She chose nurturing tea and we listened to some gentle piano music. My room is very gentle, with big windows overlooking the sea, and a soft and soothing atmosphere. I lit some candles and placed them around the room.

Because Karen was feeling disconnected from her who she really was, I asked her to begin flicking through the magazines and tear out absolutely any words, colours, pictures, images of anything that she felt would nurture and soothe her right now. Once she began she could not stop. She cut out pictures of women lying on deserted beaches, brightly coloured clothes with vibrant patterns, she cut out words like *revitalise, unwind* and *soothe your soul*. She cut out lots of images of homes that inspired her, filled with wood and natural textures. She cut out pictures of tree-filled forests and soothing seascapes. Lots of images had water in them, and there were beautiful images of women being pampered and cleansed. She cut out romantic images of couples kissing and cuddling. I could see her physically unwind, and it was wonderful to watch.

There were lots of trends appearing in the images — the outdoors was very dominant, there were lots of healing images and there were romantic desires. Although Karen couldn't verbalize what she needed in her life right now, the images revealed the deep desires and yearnings of her soul and spirit.

THE PROBLEM

When our spirits are crushed underneath the stress and pressure of our busy everyday lives, we can become so disillusioned by our day-to-day existence. It can often feel like our lives are a treadmill that offers no STOP button. I feel that the stress and the pressure can squash the essence of who we are and what we would love our lives to be like, until one day we wake up and we feel so far removed from who we are that we can't even remember what it is that we want to make us happy.

When we are so out of the habit of being who we were born to be, we just operate as a collection of bone and muscle under a layer of skin doing life instead of living it to the full. This feeling of disconnection can be daunting, and unless you have a basic awareness of how the mechanics of the mind affects our emotions, so often the only solution to numb the pain of our existence is by suppressing our emotions, and we can only hope that the feelings will go away.

I clearly remember this feeling from when I had

postnatal depression. I would wake up each day feeling as if life was a black hole. I lost sight of my creativity and my dreams, There was nothing in my life that I was looking forward to. The day became a cycle of morning and night. I look back now upon the situation and reflect on the feelings and emotions that I was experiencing. I felt locked into my own little world. I didn't complain to anyone. I didn't even know that anything was seriously wrong. To the outside world I painted on a face and acted as if everything was okay — I didn't want anyone to know that I wasn't coping. Anti-depressants were the next option. Thank God I managed to attend a Louise L. Hay workshop that offered me a new lease of life. I was free to see the future again. Even as I write this I feel so grateful for that day.

So no matter how we are feeling, there are always solutions; we just need to find them and with some gentle re-adjustments we can slowly begin to re-introduce, little by little, the much-needed joy back into our lives.

So what did Karen do next? Karen now had a

treasure map of what she really wanted in her life to begin on her gentle path of rediscovering joy. She had some big signposts that were telling her what she needed on an intuitive level.

It was quite unusual for me to watch what happened next. Karen saw the signs, and that was just what she needed to get her kick started. She posted all of the images into a journal that she read daily. She fed her imagination the images that she needed to get back on track. She booked herself a spa weekend in the country and did lots of walking; she indulged in therapies and generally unwound. When she returned home, she began to go out with her camera to the forest at weekends and took up photography again (something that she hadn't done for years). On weekends she also made sure to build in some constructive family time. Her family loved it — and so did her clients as her sense of fulfilment began to come back at work, too.

Four months after our last session, I gave her a courtesy call. She was delighted to hear from me. She said that she had begun doing a journal of all of her thoughts and feelings each day, and this kept her clear and on track. She said that her relationship with her husband had gone from strength to strength, and the affair had been only in her mind. She realized that she had resented her husband for living his life and her resentment had built up to such a level that he felt he had to lie about nights out and working late to avoid arguments with her. She was making real time for herself now, and her joy and gratitude for life had been realigned. She had begun to feel a deep connection spiritually as she engaged with nature, something that she hadn't done for so long!

In Karen's case, she knew how to do the mental work and it was just a matter of finding the soul map that would offer her insights into what would make her happy again. Even if you don't have a great knowledge of self-help, this work is a fantastic way to begin to connect you back into who you are again. Sometimes we just need to stop mentally trying to make changes and relax ...

THE CONSULTATION

When self-help doesn't work!

Sometimes the personal development work in self-help books or magazine articles that should enhance our lives and make us feel so much better and fulfilled can have the opposite effect! It can make us feel even more tired and exhausted than when we first started, especially when we feel that we can't crack something, and that nothing is really changing even though we really do want to be happy, more creative, and more in touch with who we really are.

It's a fact that making life changes is tough. It takes hard work and effort, and added on top of your existing stress it's so easy to start off with fantastic enthusiasm. However, once you begin to work the chapters or the exercises, the miraculous changes that you crave can feel like they are never going to happen. When we feel like this, it can seem like this process is just something else to add to our list of things that we have started but haven't managed to complete. This adds even more stress to our lives!!!

Your self-help guide may find itself in a pile beside all the other half-read books, or it may just gather dust underneath your bed ... soon it becomes another fad that we don't carry through. I have done it and I still do! How many magazine articles or self-development books have you read and thought *I must do that*, turned yet another page and then ... somehow the idea slips from your mind, everyday life kicks in and you are back to square one again? If this is you, then this section may be just what you need.

You may be someone who persists with the exercises with full enthusiasm and commitment but you feel that you are getting nowhere, the scars are deep and they seem to refuse to fade. If this is in any way how you feel, then this section offers you an alternative route to happiness, joy and freedom. It is the ULTIMATE stress reliever and soul and spirit connection and a healing strategy to help move you to inner wellness.

Connecting to your creativity

Through coaching and training hundreds of people on making positive life changes and building self-esteem, I have found some very interesting trends when people feel anxious, stressed and out of balance with their lives.

The main one is that the majority of people that I meet feel that they have lost the connection with themselves! If this sounds odd, what I mean is their spirit, or their sense of who they are and what they love and what they would love to do with their lives, has been dulled or numbed by their life experiences or just the sheer hard work of living.

As I begin to work with them, it's as if their internal light is not on. I have found that when they begin to recharge their self-esteem, to love and respect themselves, to forgive themselves and others, to accept that they are deserving of happiness and joy, they can begin to reconnect with the joy of life. If the usual techniques can't get through, and we want to find another way to connect up with our innate wellbeing, I do some soul and spirit excavation. Once we tap into the joy that lies at the core of your inner world, we can begin to release some positive feelings and emotions. Before we do this, we need to appreciate that our minds and bodies and spirit are connected.

Understanding the mind—body link!

It is now a widely recognised fact that the mind and the body are intrinsically linked (psycho-neuro-immunology). What this means is that whatever is going on in our minds or our hearts is having an impact on our bodies. The mind has the ability to heal us or to kill us — when we feed our minds with feelings of willingness, openness, joy, positive stimulation and interest, when we feel that we are fulfilling a purpose, when we are learning and growing in mind and spirit, we feel connected and fulfilled in life.

Alternatively, when we feel exhausted from not enough sleep; when we don't take regular exercise; when we take in too many stimulants; when we eat badly; when we never stop to reflect and review our lives; when we feel that we have no sense of purpose; when we feel lonely, angry, resentful, despondent and we feel that there is no love in our lives, both for ourselves and others, we can feel that life is so heavy and we don't know where to start to connect into our joy and happiness. When we fill our minds up with our creativity and self-love and respect, this boosts our immune systems, and our feelings of wellbeing and joy are enhanced.

Conversely, if we trap our minds with negative reinforcements, when we feel trapped, frightened, and without any kind of purpose, we can feel weighed down by the pressures of life.

THE PRESCRIPTION

In my book *Zest for Life* and in my workshops that are now run all over the world, I offer in great detail a process to achieving your dreams and ambitions. One of the tools in the book is the creativity journal, the technique that I used with Karen at the beginining of this chapter. It has been designed to take minimum effort to create and even if you feel flat and exhausted, this lovely project is what I feel will help you to begin to pour some colour, creativity and purpose back into your world.

The way that the creativity journal works is that it focuses on the way you would love your life to be; it digs into your inner yearnings and through the creative process it stimulates your creativity, your positive thoughts and your imagination. By doing all of these, it feeds your mind pictures of possibility and hope, something that you may have been missing for a while. Your inner blocks may have sucked out all of your energy, inspiration, positivity, belief and inspiration from your life. The images in the creativity journal are devoured by your subconscious mind, and over a period of time (especially if you pop the images into a journal or scrap book on your pillow and look at it every night), this results in a subtle refocusing of your thoughts and your destiny; it feeds your spirit and your immune system to boost you back to life again.

The Creativity Journal
(let's shine a torch on your soul!)

What you will need:

- Six magazines (spend a little bit extra on inspirational ones and include holiday brochures and Sunday magazines)
- A big glass/bottle of your favourite wine or a totally indulgent smoothie
- A big scrap book (preferably with at least 20 pages – you MUST like the look and feel of it)
- A glue stick

Create some time for yourself when you are not going to be interrupted. Put on some relaxing and soothing music, light some candles and pour yourself a gorgeous glass of something ...

When you are totally relaxed, begin by choosing some different headings for your journal (maybe four to start with). Choose the headings/words that seem to resonate with you and immediately offer you a lovely feeling. Choose from the following:

Love
Relationships
Connection
Relaxing and soothing ideas
Looking and feeling great
Creative activities
Energizing ideas
Fun things for free
Wild adventures
Wonderful weekend breaks
The new me!
Feeling fantastic
My wonderful home

Once you have chosen your headings, begin to flick through the magazines and brochures to find out what images and words match your wildest desires. Don't worry about sticking images in the book that are beyond your wildest dreams, just begin to build a treasure map of the yearnings of your heart and soul. Cut out images of things that would heal your bruised spirit.

Each evening ponder the images, and consider how you can, step by step, in little ways, move towards your inner desires and needs. This is the repair journey to happiness and contentment. If you really would like to explore the process of achieving these dreams, pick up a copy of my book *Zest for Life* and work through the process to living your wildest dreams.

The Gratitude Ritual

Take the TIME to be THANKFUL for all that is in your WORLD ...

This is another fantastic practical tool for refocusing a negative, worn-out, exhausted mind. By using this every day, we can begin to think of all the reasons we are happy to be alive. The gratitude ritual gently awakens possibility and hope in our minds and lets us see that even when things are challenging and difficult, beneath the surface there are always reasons to be happy and grateful. Often the dark clouds of gloom obscure the joy that is going on in our lives.

When you lie in bed tonight, think back over the past few weeks. Think of friends, family, colleagues and the setting in which you live. Are you grateful for your relationships, your home, the fact that you can pay your bills, how you are and your children's health? What other reasons do you have to be grateful? Take a moment to think of the difficulties in other people's lives, and count your blessings for the simple things in your life.

The Ritual

Each morning or evening, light a candle and count your blessings; be grateful for the things that you DO have in your life.

Write a list each day of 10 reasons to be grateful. At the end of 21 days, read what you have written – and then let it all go. Check out what happens in your mind and body when you look at the reasons you have to be grateful. This exercise can help to release energy on a physical level.

When we are focused on gratefulness, our lives feel completely different. Often this gratefulness opens us up to a deeper spiritual connection as we are receptive to the boundless opportunities that the universe offers us. Each day we are presented with opportunities for growth and joy, however depending on where your focus is, this will determine whether you see the opportunities or not.

Work on changing your perceptions and watch the opportunities flood into your life. You only need to read the preceding chapters in this book to realise how your thoughts have the power to block out your joy in life.

Walking, LISTENING or writing for answers!

Going DEEPER ...

Each morning, before anyone gets up, I sit down and light my candle and do my gratitude work. I always make sure that I am really comfortable and that I am not going to be disturbed ... I close my eyes, take a few deep breaths and relax. I connect deeply with my intuition (source), and I ask the questions, big or small, that need to be answered for the day ahead.

When I listen deeply for answers and I ask what to do next ... solutions begin to come. I guess you may call this ritual meditation or prayer. Either way, with practice it works, and I am left with a feeling of peace, calm, and hope, as I feel connected to my source.

Some days I go for walks and practise this same ritual (with my eyes open but my mind focused!) and again when I do, the voice in my mind begins to come up with the answers that I need to hear ... This is a fantastic feeling, and when we are caught up in the storm of life and we cannot work out what to do next, it gives us access to the answers that lie beneath the surface.

Another option for soul or intuition excavation is to get up each day and do some journaling. In her bestselling book, *The Artist's Way*, Julia Cameron teaches us to do our morning pages. She suggests that by writing down our thoughts for fifteen minutes each morning, we can begin to make headway through our storm and address the real issues that are going on in our lives. Our thoughts, hopes and fears may be revealed in our random writings to reveal so much about where we are in our minds. After reading your pages after 21 days, you may begin to see some trends in your ramblings that you can act on.

Another alternative to working with the morning pages would be to ask for some guidance in your life and listen to your intuition (source) feed back the answers to you. I always find it amazing how we can learn so much from the knowledge that comes back to us through these words ... Often I am amazed at the words on my page, as I realise they are the words of something much greater than I am!

I know that personally, this is the feeling that plugs me into the universe, and somehow the considered answers that come back for me remind me that I am not alone in this big world. Again try this for 21 days ... you might be amazed at what you find.

When we realize that the world is actually a good

place and that the universe (our source) is working for us and not against us, we can feel a great sense of joy and connection. We feel alive and safe in a place where life has possibilities and hope. There is no doubt that these processes take hard work and effort and a bit of time to evolve, however I promise you – from someone who has been there – it's well worth the effort.

Affirmations to help you connect with your sense of self again

Make a list of affirmations and support them with some powerful accelerators/statements or points that support your affirmation and make it more believable. Following are some examples of the types of accelerators you might want to use to support your affirmation.

- Compliments that you have received
- The goal that drives you to think your thought

- Reminders from your past when you thought this way
- Common-sense reasons to believe this thought

Make sure that you read them every day until you feel different and people begin to treat you differently.

I love life; today I make time
to do one thing just for me.
'Me time' energizes me,
I need 'me time' to recharge
my soul so that I can offer
even more to others.
When I look after me,
I have so much more to
offer others.

My life is an exciting adventure.
From today on I MAKE time for me.
Playing with life boosts my
immune system and makes
me feel so much healthier and
happier.

My life is important;
I am a special human being.

Today I choose to say
yes to life; in turn,
opportunities will
now choose me.

Life is an adventure
or nothing at all.

I allow my creativity
to run wild; this fills me
up with joy.

Signing off ...

IN THE time since I started this book, I have adopted a new cat. He just arrived one evening in our garden when I was relaxing my fingers and my bones after a whole day of writing. I met him as he was teasing some of our little frogs in our pond (poor frogs, but God, can our frogs jump ... the cat doesn't stand a chance!). I have called him Tigger. I call him that because he looks like a gorgeous little tiger cub. He has sat at my feet or on my desk as I have written for almost ten hours for the last thirty days and has been the most amazing little companion. He's sprawled out on the floor at my feet right now.

Each night at about nine o'clock I have popped him outside, as Liberty's little hamster 'Hammy' wakes up for the night! Hammy also sits on my desk, and I have been paying lots of attention to him as our new member of the family skulks around looking for food! (Oh dear!)

It's gorgeous here at this wonderful house, and every day I count my blessings. I dreamed it would be this way once ... and here I am! For me, my soul medicine is my comfortable home, having my family and friends and animals around.

I have loads of little sideline hobbies like restoring furniture and mosaicing pots – I love doing creative things even though it's a bit debatable how good I am! (Who cares? I love it!) All these things keep me busy when I'm not out there in the media doing my campaigning work on the importance or raising the awareness of positive self-esteem.

As you may imagine, I love my life. However, as you have flicked through the pages of this book, you are probably aware that things haven't always been this rosy. I have made self-development a passion and I guess something of an obsession, and as a result I have spent the last ten years working on me. The result of the obsession is that I am in the place of my dreams today. It's been a very bumpy ride and

I still have off days; however, I feel pretty contented and unblocked. Life feels pretty groovy in this place right now, and I now feel that as things come up in the future, as they surely will, I have a range of tools and techniques to help guide me through.

I have the same dream for you. I may not know you, however I have written this book for you in the hope that you have access to the best of the tools and techniques that I have learned so far. Now that you have this little book in your hands, know and understand that the theory is not enough – the answers are in persevering with the exercises and the affirmations until you begin to feel different inside.

If then they don't work, please seek further professional help. What a waste of a life if you don't – please make the commitment for you, if you do, there could be love, happiness and abundance around the next corner for you. Just take a peek into your mind for a moment of the way you would love your life to be in your wildest dreams. Paint the picture

– what do you really want?

Good luck and lots of love to you on your journey, you precious grain of sparkle dust.

Until the next time ...
Dawn xx

Further resources

Life coaching

Life coaching is ideal if you feel that you keep getting into bad habits when you go for your goals. It is future-focused and does not delve into your past.

If you know that you need a helping hand to move in the direction of your dreams, life coaching can be fantastic. Make sure that you find a specialist life coach who has a wide knowledge and experience in whatever area you want to explore – for example careers, relationships, self-esteem, etc. General life coaching qualifications do not focus on training in specialist areas, so always ask where the coach's expertise lies. You should always take the opportunity of trying out a free session or have a good long chat with your coach before committing.

Speak free to one of my specialist coaches at **www.dawnbreslin.com.**

NHS counselling (UK only)

This is a free service, with a waiting list, but in the meantime, to get you started, pick up some self-help books from a bookstore or library. You will be referred to a counsellor, but remember that if you feel he/she does not work for you, ask to change – you must feel comfortable with your counsellor, and a good working relationship is essential for you to achieve the right result. It's a great opportunity to begin to address the issues that continue to hold you back from your authentic happiness in life. Remember, NHS counselling is short-term; however it will offer you a real insight for the type of help you may need in the longer term.

Workshops

Workshops are a fantastic place to learn, share, develop and grow. Sometimes to go through the experience of realization and releasing emotion with people that you will never see again can be quite liberating. Don't be afraid that you are the only person in the room who needs help. I always find it so interesting how everyone is in the same boat as me; we've just had different variations on the same type of problems. This is my preferred learning environment. Once again, make sure that you connect with the teacher/workshop leader before you sign up. It's essential that there is mutual respect to encourage growth and development. Check out what's happening in your local area and look on the Internet for national/international workshops. For example:

Dawn Breslin workshops @ www.dawnbreslin.com
SARK workshops visit www.campsark.com (USA)

Charities and agencies dealing with specific issues

Many charities, voluntary organisations and agencies offer counselling and support groups on specific subjects, e.g., Alcoholics Anonymous, Rape Crisis, Cancer Care, Women's Aid, – again, check out your local area for details. Psychotherapy aims to help the person as a whole rather than concentrating on a particular symptom or issue. There are many overlaps between counselling and therapy, and both can feel intense, but therapy tends to go deeper, takes longer and has a longer-lasting effect. Most therapists offer a free introductory meeting to give you the opportunity to get a sense of whether you would be able to work together. It's essential to get the right therapist, so ask about their training, experience, supervision, ethical code, special skills and areas of interest. Ask yourself if it's important for you to see a man or a woman. The initial interview is for you to meet and check out what is important for you, and for you to get a feel for each other. If you don't feel comfortable, find someone you feel at ease with.

Magazines

There are many magazines on the stands that feature both orthodox and alternative medical advice. Check them out for cutting-edge tips on health and wellbeing.

Books and audio CDs

Visit your local bookstore, one of the chains if possible, to browse the huge and ever-growing range of self-development/popular psychology books to choose from. Or check out **Amazon.com** and search for specific subject areas. There are some specific books that can assist you on your journey of development. Here is a list of fantastic titles for starters.

General self-awareness
Zest for Life by Dawn Breslin

Fears
Feel the Fear and Do it Anyway by Susan Jeffers

Creativity/therapeutic self-development
SARK's Journal and Playbook by Sark

Creativity/soul recovery
The Artist's Way by Julia Cameron

Self-esteem
You Can Heal Your Life by Louise L. Hay

Healing therapies
Healing without Freud and Prozac by
Dr. David Servan-Schreiber

Healing cancer
Love, Medicine and Miracles by Dr. Bernie Siegel

Spiritual connection
The Celestine Prophecy by James Redfield

CD (general)
Everyday Wisdom by Dr. Wayne W. Dyer

Also by Dawn Breslin

"Dawn Breslin is one of the top teachers around today."
—**Louise Hay**

A practical, interactive workbook that will help even the most cynical individual unlock creativity, add sparkle to life, boost self-confidence and move on from simply existing to bouncing out of bed each day!

Available from all good bookstores or by contacting Hay House (see last page).

Hay House Titles of Related Interest

The Best Year of Your Life Kit, by Debbie Ford

Empowering Women, by Louise L. Hay

Empowerment Cards, by Tavis Smiley

Everything I've Ever Done That Worked,
by Lesley Garner

Five Steps for Overcoming Fear and Self-Doubt,
by Wyatt Webb

The Power of Intention, by Dr. Wayne W. Dyer

Soul Coaching, by Denise Linn

All of the above are available at your local
bookstore, or may be ordered by visiting:
Hay House USA: **www.hayhouse.com;** Hay House
Australia: **www.hayhouse.com.au;** Hay House UK:
www.hayhouse.co.uk; Hay House South Africa:
orders@psdprom.co.za

Dawn Breslin Workshops and Training Programmes

Zest for Life – Discover Your True Potential

This programme has been designed to gently take you by the hand on a journey to self-discovery from childhood to the present moment and beyond to a fabulous future. *Zest for Life* workshops present a great opportunity to revise your dreams and ambitions, unlock your potential and inspire you to live the life you dream of!

- Change your mindset from 'simply existing' to 'really living'
- Identify and overcome your limiting beliefs
- Renew your inspiration and conquer your fears
- Build up your confidence and rediscover your creativity
- Release your true potential
- Create a solid, focused and personal vision
- Create a compelling and achievable life plan

Fast Track Your Potential –
Maximizing Human Potential

Our Fast Track Your Potential Programme is an inspirational intensive training session that has been described as a nine-hour personal coaching experience, taking delegates through an exciting programme of self-discovery, motivation, focus and change. This unique and personal course enables individuals to rediscover life balance and revise their working life ambitions.

- Move beyond your restrictive limitations
- Increase your self-esteem and confidence
- Unlock your true potential
- Create a solid life plan
- Identify and overcome fears

Training Academy

If you are an experienced coach or trainer and would like to train on one of the current Dawn Breslin Workshops, the Dawn Breslin Training Academy provides you with the opportunity to learn new skills in personal development and offers a range of ready-made programmes to your client base.

We are looking for talented individuals who have:
- An incredible passion for personal development
- The ability to motivate, inspire and develop individuals to achieve their dreams and ultimate aspirations
- Excellent communication skills

If you would like to attend any of the Dawn Breslin Programmes or would like further information, please e-mail the Dawn Breslin Team at: info@dawnbreslin.com

---

Every so often, right in the middle of an
ordinary life, inspiration comes along,
and life is a fairytale ...

We hope you enjoyed this Hay House book.
If you'd like to receive a free catalog featuring additional
Hay House books and products, or if you'd like information about the
Hay Foundation, please contact:

Hay House, Inc.
P.O. Box 5100
Carlsbad, CA 92018-5100

(760) 431-7695 or **(800) 654-5126**
(760) 431-6948 (fax) or **(800) 650-5115 (fax)**
www.hayhouse.com

• •

Published and distributed in Australia by: Hay House Australia Pty. Ltd. • 18/36 Ralph St. •
Alexandria NSW 2015 • *Phone:* 612-9669-4299 •
Fax: 612-9669-4144 • www.hayhouse.com.au

Published and distributed in the United Kingdom by:
Hay House UK, Ltd. • Unit 62, Canalot Studios •
222 Kensal Rd., London W10 5BN • *Phone:* 44-20-8962-1230
Fax: 44-20-8962-1239 • www.hayhouse.co.uk

Published and distributed in the Republic of South Africa by:
Hay House SA (Pty), Ltd., P.O. Box 990, Witkoppen 2068
Phone/Fax: 27-11-706-6612 • orders@psdprom.co.za

Distributed in Canada by: Raincoast • 9050 Shaughnessy St., Vancouver, B.C. V6P 6E5 •
Phone: (604) 323-7100 • *Fax:* (604) 323-2600

• •

Tune in to **www.hayhouseradio.com™** for the best in inspirational talk radio featuring top
Hay House authors! And, sign up via the Hay House USA Website to receive the Hay House
online newsletter and stay informed about what's going on with your favorite authors.
You'll receive bimonthly announcements about: Discounts and Offers,
Special Events, Product Highlights, Free Excerpts, Giveaways, and more!
www.hayhouse.com